ctly from the con
others has sprun
is 'green' architec
suringly expressiv
he monumental —
nues to define Aus
, plastic and ofte
s object; and con
s rendered distinc

THE AUSTRALIAN HOUSE

Anna Johnson
Patrick Bingham-Hall

CONTENTS

27 **Adey House**
Ashton Raggatt McDougall

35 **Applecross House**
Jackson Clements Burrows

43 **Barro House**
Wood Marsh

53 **Bastian Farm-House**
Troppo Architects

65 **Bellevue Hill House**
Marsh Cashman Koolloos Architects

73 **Bondi Wave House**
Tony Owen NDM

81 **Box House**
Neeson Murcutt Architects

89 **Brett's House**
Rosevear Architects

97 **Brookes Street House**
James Russell Architect

109 **Cape Schanck House**
Paul Morgan Architects

119 **Cape Schanck House & Studio**
Denton Corker Marshall

129 **Coldstream Residence**
Allan Powell Architects

139 **Eyelid House**
Fiona Winzar Architects

147 **Folded House**
Dale Jones-Evans Architecture

155 **Garden House**
Peter Stutchbury Architecture

165 **Gidgegannup Residence**
iredale pedersen hook architects

175	**The Great Wall of Warburton** BKK Architects	339	**Rowntree Street House** Rex Addison - Addison Associates
185	**Highgate Hill Residence** Richard Kirk Architect	349	**Springwater** Peter Stutchbury Architecture
195	**Holman House** Durbach Block Architects	359	**Spry House** Durbach Block Architects
207	**House 42** Dimitty Andersen Architects	369	**Stanwell Park House** Casey Brown Architecture
217	**House of Orange** Elizabeth Watson-Brown Architects	381	**Swan Street Residence** iredale pedersen hook architects
227	**Ivanhoe House** Kerstin Thompson Architects	391	**Tibet Gallery** Donovan Hill
239	**James Robertson House** Casey Brown Architecture	401	**Tyson Street House** Jackson Clements Burrows
249	**Klein Bottle House** McBride Charles Ryan	411	**Vineyard House** John Wardle Architects
261	**Leura House** James Stockwell Architect	423	**Wallaby Way House** Troppo Architects Queensland
273	**Machans Beach Cottage** Deb Fisher - Fisher Buttrose Architects	433	**Whale Beach** Alex Popov Architects
283	**Na's House** Elizabeth Watson-Brown Architects	445	**Wheatsheaf House** Jesse Judd - Judd Lysenko Marshall
293	**Narveno Court House** McBride Charles Ryan	455	**Winter Cottage** Chindarsi Architects
303	**Northbridge House** Alex Popov Architects	467	**(w)right House** Charles Wright Architects
311	**Perham Residence** Simon Hanson - Bureau SRH	479	**Zulaikha Laurence House** Tonkin Zulaikha Greer with Drew Heath
319	**Point Piper House** Louise Nettleton Architects	490	houses
329	**Rosebery House** Andresen O'Gorman	494	architects

THE AUSTRALIAN HOUSE
by anna johnson

Recent Australian architecture has been defined by the growing awareness of the implications of global warming, with the attendant need for new buildings to address this reality. Whilst sustainable place-making has been practised by some architects for several decades, such responsibility is now unavoidable, and the discipline of architecture is being determined by this new reality.

This imperative has triggered a range of investigations of technical inventions and implementations, as well as an examination of a series of strategies that extend beyond the architectural envelope itself to the broader community and surrounding infrastructure. Some recent Australian house designs emerge directly from the context of the site, whilst the formal expression of many others has sprung from a rethinking of what environmentally-conscious 'green' architecture should look like… and the new forms are reassuringly expressive and defiant. A marked emphasis upon the theme of the monumental – a return to the idea of 'architecture as object' – continues to define Australia's domestic architecture. *Form:* typically dense, plastic and often massive, is resolved and expressed as an autonomous object; and *context,* rather than being synthesized or embodied, is rendered distinct and separate through its juxtaposition with the monumental. This is not to deny the significance of context, but other ideas of relationship have been brought into play, as new and alternative readings of context and building arise through this configuration. Alterations and additions now feature extensively in architectural practice, and the formal devices demonstrate similar expressive tectonics. The informative role that the context and the existing buildings play in the evolution of the new structure is of particular interest in these projects.

In addition to the concerns of sustainability, there are two central points of origin for the renewed interest in 'architecture as object'… both with roots in the Modernist project. One – characterized by orthogonal cubic geometries, planar surfaces and pavilion hybrids – has a direct lineage to the high modernist period, from Le Corbusier to the International Style, and especially to the Californian Case Study Houses. The second category – expressionist and experimental in form, and more regionally particular – continues a trajectory coming out of the European *avant-garde* of the 20th century: from German expressionism and Russian constructivism, through to Alvar Aalto, José Coderch, Hans Scharoun, Eero Saarinen, and the later works of Le Corbusier.

Aside from the investment in form, materiality, boundaries, relationships of interior to exterior, and a particular affluence… certain consistencies of approach and exploration can be seen across a range of recent Australian houses, and a further series of commonalities emerge. In contrast to the plasticity of the forms – whether monumental, abstracted or expressionist – the materiality expresses a density and *gravitas*. Whether built from masonry, timber, rammed-earth or concrete, the surface becomes an unadorned skin – hermetic and often impenetrable – and no longer characteristic of the late 20th century perceptions of Australian architecture. This new work emerges from a certain worldly affluence – both economic and intellectual – and many of the houses do not speak specifically of a regional architecture… their context is as much international as it is national. And when the dialogue does engage with local histories and context, it is strongly grounded in international precedents and dialogue.

Sustainable architecture: the new imperative

Sustainability and 'green' architecture are, of course, by no means new, but the reality of global warming could well define 21st century politics, culture and society, and the necessity to rethink consumption, behavioural patterns and ways of life has – in particular – dramatically altered architecture's relationship to the environment. The projects illustrated in this book express several alternative directions… all the houses accommodate basic environmental, climatic and solar requirements, and in some cases – like Joe Chindarsi's exquisite cabinet-like Winter Cottage (*right*) in Western Australia – sustainability is the central preoccupation. This collection of houses displays the work of architects who have a serious investment in sustainable place-making and in building responsible architecture for the Australian context.

At one level, environmental concerns have led to investigations of the image and the appearance of 'green' architecture. What should these buildings look like, and what should they feel like? Charles Wright – in Port Douglas at the northern extreme of the continent – and Paul Morgan – at Cape Schanck on the southern tip – have designed houses that are fundamentally environmentally-responsive, whilst proposing a radical rethink of the aesthetics of such architecture. Both architects employ contemporary processes of architectural technology and digital representation, which have inspired highly figurative buildings… startling in their divergence from commonly held perceptions of sustainable site-specific architecture.

Sustainability has come to have an increasing broad and ephemeral meaning, referring to a myriad of ideologies and technologies. For Deb Fisher and Elizabeth Watson-Brown, sustainability is as concerned with the social and the cultural potential of architecture as it is with building technologies. Central to their architecture are issues of reuse, and of place-making that involves careful consideration of contextual social conditions, local identity, patterns of usage, and habits formed over time, rather than formal architectural expressions and traditional notions of architectural tectonics. Dwelling is thus not defined by the architectural envelope *per se*, but rather by a series of relationships, passages and 'felt experiences' that the building – and systems of pathways, landscaping and programs – can orchestrate.

For some architects, such as Iredale Pederson Hook, the idea of sustainability extends to an investigation of the suburb and its contextual social and community networks. Through forensic analysis of the suburb and specific adjacent conditions, a series of tools and strategies are derived for regenerating an existing condition. And whilst form is almost secondary for Watson-Brown and Fisher, form (and its origin) is essential for Iredale Pedersen Hook, and their architecture – formally rich with expressive gestures and material selections – is programmatically inventive in its reconfiguration.

Abstract monumentalism: the house and context

Architecture as a sculptural, monumental object - of both symbolic and visceral intent – has its historical antecedents in the shaping of civic space, and allied to this role was the unequivocal demarcation between the *gravitas* of the civic realm and the mundane domestic reality. Modernism altered this. One of the key and lasting provocations of modernism was the appropriation of the elements and devices of civic monumentality from a wide and diverse range of programs – factories, workers clubs, theatres and incinerators – and, critically, the house. From the end of the 19th century, and most notably in the early 20th century, the modernist program found increasing expression through, and identification with, the private dwelling. The burgeoning middle class, with its affluence and its appetites, proved a persuasive and liberal partner.

Precedents for this 'monumental' approach within the body of 20th century Australian architecture are generally exceptions to the dominant trends, rather than the rule. The particular and confident assertion of monumental, abstract, and frequently expressionist houses is a more recent development. A striking aspect of many of these projects hinges on ideas of legibility and identity, as many of these houses do not look like houses, as houses may be typically read and understood. They present themselves with an equally defined exterior and interior, which do not always follow as one from the other. Ambiguity is common, with an external masking of the location of the entrance, or even the exact nature of the building. This is further amplified by abstracted and sculptural qualities, even further divorced from the usual and reassuring signifiers of dwelling. With many of the 'new' houses, the appearance of the house from the street disguises the extraordinary spatial and formal gymnastics that unfold within. These delights are saved for the inhabitants and their visitors: a private experience not to be claimed by surrounding onlookers. Many of the houses have unassuming, decidedly modest frontages, and whilst this is partially a result of various planning and heritage regimes, the architectural strategy is intentional, and this ambiguity serves to heighten the sculptural and abstracted qualities of the houses.

This phenomenon is not specific to urban settings, as idyllic rural and coastal sites have become another location for such experiments. The approach on these sites is the most spectacular, thus challenging the assumption of an Australian architecture that should 'touch the earth lightly', merging as a 'non-object' into its context. The Klein Bottle House by McBride Charles Ryan and the Cape Schanck House and Studio by Denton Corker Marshall (both set against the tea trees of the Mornington Peninsula) are startling examples. Abstractions floating against the coastal landscape, these houses recall neither the ubiquitous beach shack nor the adjacent 'architectural' houses where roofs mimic the undulations of dunes and waves. Through this strategy of placing an abstraction onto the landscape, one's attention is drawn to the particularities of the site. These houses are not alien insertions without regard for context, but their methodology and approach aspires to a different experience and sensorial response. Through dissimilarity and otherness, the context becomes heightened… thrown into relief.

Redefined boundaries: exterior as object, interior as dwelling

Legibility is further tested and provoked through experiments with scale – or, to be precise, 'scalelessness' – where the object emerges from a manipulation of form and material that could exist at a range of scales, resulting from explorations not initially dependent on program. Dale Jones-Evans uses the term 'origami', McBride Charles Ryan *(Klein Bottle House, right)* quote the 'pixel', and Wood Marsh the 'fold' in their discussions of process and origin. All these terms imply the 'miniature' and the 'delicate'. The architecture is thus the action of re-scaling – and over-scaling – that original gesture. This manoeuvre is not quite that of the postmodernist artist or architect – such as Claes Oldenberg or Robert Venturi – as the intent is located in the potential of form itself: in the gesture rather than the symbol. More like dress-making than pop art, this is a process of finessing the three-dimensional resolution and expression… the focus is on that gesture, and not on the crafting of a highly refined object, where structure, detailing and materiality are an end in themselves.

The intent – the 'meaning' – has more to do with abstraction, as the object in totality relies on sensorial and experiential engagement, rather than a comprehension dependent on linguistic or referential signifiers. And, in doing so, these buildings achieve a unity and a completeness of gesture. At the same time, there is an obvious intellectual richness to the work and to the process of form-making and planning with which the architects have engaged. Although much of the architecture emanating from these manipulations is seen in the public realm, its application at a domestic 'scale' is – in many ways – more intriguing, as the results are so unexpected in their suburban or rural context. The concerns of these Australian architects are deeply anchored in cultural and architectural histories and precedents, and this architectural dialogue is markedly more international in its emphasis. Even when regional concerns and a local architecture are necessarily relevant, the architecture is always cognisant of and engaged with broader architectural discussions.

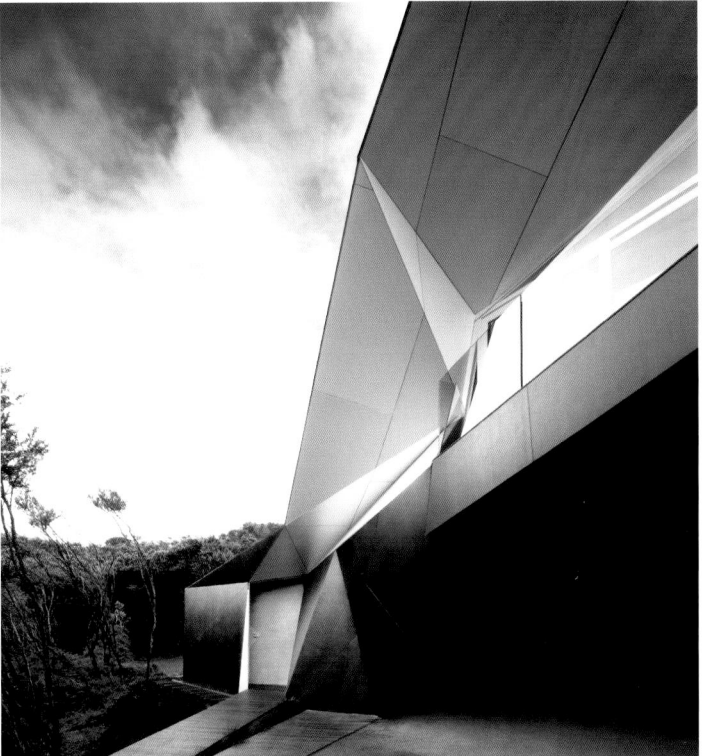

The interior: ritual and the domestic realm

For many architects, boundaries and thresholds have been reinvested with new emphasis, and 'interiority' in their houses is allowed its own unique identity: a separate, and alternative, formal and spatial presence to that of the enclosing container. Lacking a seamless transition between inside and outside, these houses often emphasise separation and distinction. Within, whether plastic and malleable, or darkly atmospheric, the dialogue is not concerned with a 'blurring' between interior and exterior, but with the assertion of two distinct architectural experiences. What determines the interior – aside from airflow, sun-angle and view requirements – is a domestic narrative reinvested with ideas of ritual and layered spatial progressions. For example, in a manner reminiscent of 'old world' configurations, the experience of passage is not always a linear and direct one. The passage is now ritualistic and

episodic, directed by movement past thresholds of entry, through and into differing domestic territories. The 'journey' takes on a new importance, or a regained importance, engaging a mode of dwelling that shifts across a series of domestic territories and imaginative acts. This sense of passage through and into, recalls the primacy of the idea of an architecturally mediated journey from the familiar into something removed and 'other'.

Allan Powell asserts this difference particularly clearly… the interior of his Coldstream House describes a narrative quite distinct from that of the exterior, which presents an intriguing antidote to the prevalence of the 'view' in much Australian architecture. Powell directs the viewer inwards, and the most powerful space is a dark gallery that runs the entire length of the house. Alternatively, the Machans Beach Cottage, by Deb Fisher, possesses a fluid indoor and outdoor 'interior', as the domestic realm expands to include the garden, and the spatial journey moves through discrete thresholds from the street to the house, from the house into the garden, and then back into the house. Similarly, Kerstin Thompson's Ivanhoe House explores the possibility of a looping internal progression that circulates around a central courtyard and through various domestic programs.

Sculptural expressionism: a new plasticity

'Monumentalism' as an idea is experienced in many of these houses: it denotes a sense of density and mass, and it is liberated and animated by an expressionist plasticity of form. Almost without exception, this direction is characterized by non-orthogonal, non-Cartesian geometries. John Wardle's buildings, twisting in plan, have a suppleness and muscularity about them, as if they were composed of flesh and had a bodily presence. His Vineyard House *(left)* expresses a sleek animation and formal agility, anchored to the landscape by a massive rammed-earth wall. Malleable swooping interior forms burst out of the floating pavilions of the Leura House by James Stockwell, which are likewise grounded by rammed-earth walls. The fluid waves (in masonry) of Tony Owen NDM's Bondi Wave House and the soaring scarlet curves (in steel and plywood) of Jesse Judd's Wheatsheaf House are also clear examples of this expressionist trajectory. Though representative of an entirely different genre of project and architectural lineage, Rex Addison's Rowntree Street House expresses this same plasticity of form, although the moves are preserved for the interior alone.

Another series of houses, and perhaps the most ambitious – Durbach Block's Holman House *(right)*, McBride Charles Ryan's Klein Bottle House, Wood Marsh's Barro House, Peter Stutchbury's Springwater and Denton Corker Marshall's Cape Schanck House and Studio – take this exploration of expressionist abstraction to another level. These projects display architectonics unprecedented within Australia… highly sculptural, abstract, and spatially rich, they almost defy critique. They are *bravura* projects, imbued with a singularity of resolution, and with an assertive autonomy, that define their own field of reference. Inspired by Spanish architect José Antonio Coderch's Casa Ugalde (1951), the plan of the Holman House – a weaving serpentine figure stitched across a cliff edge – describes separate 'wings' of the building, and this curvature continues in the third dimension, pushing out and away from the site. The Barro House is a similar sculptural abstraction, and whilst the language is formally resolved and representative of a singular holistic idea within the terms of the project, references from Palladio's Villa Rotunda (1566-1571) to Le Corbusier's Villa Savoye (1928-1929), are woven throughout.

Such houses have been influenced by the architecture that emerged in the later years of modernism. These works – by Coderch, Le Corbusier, Eero Saarinen, Louis Kahn and Hans Scharoun – were not representative of high modernism's reduction-

ist mantra of universality, restrictive formal palette and prescriptive social agenda: they were more regionally responsive and more experimental, both formally and structurally.

Architects who sat just outside the dominant modernist canon, such as Alvar Aalto and Rudolph Schindler, form another important reference. Although Aalto went through an early period of functionalism, by 1938 – with his Villa Mairea – he had moved away from that orthodox modernism and into what was broadly termed 'Regional Modernism'. For architects such as Durbach Block and BKK, their interest in Aalto has as much to do with his fluid, relatively expressionist forms, and in building skins that become hermetic surfaces following curved or splayed plan forms and sections, as it has to do with their regionalist agenda. Similarly Rudolph Schindler's West Hollywood Studio/Residence (1921-1922) expressed a more particular, textural and humane architecture, which has drawn the attraction of many Australian architects. With its interior structural system of exposed timber ceiling and wall members, and rich expressive detailing, Neeson Murcutt's Box House expresses such an affinity.

Another undeniable influence for this expressionist work -– shown clearly in the houses of Dale Jones-Evans, McBride Charles Ryan, Wood Marsh and Tony Owen NDM – are the theories and styles in architecture that developed, and became representative of, a certain zeitgeist in the 1990s. The French poststructuralist theoretician Gilles Deleuze, following hot on the heels of Jacques Derrida and the Deconstructivists, wrote *The Fold: Leibniz and the Baroque* in 1988. The resulting movement, embraced by artists and architects alike, (and, admittedly, uneven in rigour and quality) became known as 'Folding in Architecture'. At best, the work was conceptually and formally innovative, and sculpturally beautiful, and at worst, a paper-thin metaphorical translation of the verb 'to fold'. The influence of this movement on recent Australian house design – which also echoed German expressionist architecture – was more concerned with the architectonic language than with the theoretical position of Deleuze. Developing at a similar time to 'Folding in Architecture' were experimentations with digital technologies, which coincided with a renewed interest in mathematics and geometry, and highly complex models of behavioural patterns. Architects such as Wood Marsh, McBride Charles Ryan and Ashton Raggatt McDougall became preoccupied with a formal exploration of the type, as digital technologies – particularly three-dimensional modelling – enabled the pursuit, the testing, and the building of complex geometries and skins in a way that had not been previously accessible or economically viable at a domestic scale. These technologies also enabled abstraction to emerge as a layered totality.

New vernaculars: the heavy lightweights

The houses of Troppo, in particular, represent the continuing exploration of an Australian vernacular: a climatically responsive architecture taking precedent from traditional rural buildings; whilst Casey Brown's finely detailed and materially rich houses betray an interest in the Arts and Crafts, taking vernacular precedents to a sophisticated level, especially when coupled with ingenious planning. Another evolutionary strand of timber construction can be detected in the recent houses of a broad range of architects, which display a thematic consistency of assertive form and supple skins. One series of houses by BKK, Charles Wright and Kerstin Thompson, display expressive architectonics and a plasticity of form and space, whereby a dominant timber skin hermetically wraps a form into which openings and screens are then cut and sliced. The highly modulated timber-clad interiors and expressive exteriors of Melbourne architects Harold Desbrowe-Annear (working in the early 20th century) and Roy Grounds (working in the 1950s and 1960s) are important precedents for these houses.

Another series of houses – by Brisbane-based architects Andresen O'Gorman, Richard Kirk, Donovan Hill, James Russell and Elizabeth Watson-Brown – represents a trajectory concerned with issues of place-making in Australia, and with the very essence and qualities that timber construction can offer. Brisbane was introduced to modernist principles – specifically those of Marcel Breuer, Harry Seidler and the Case Study Houses – with the post WWII timber-clad houses of Hayes & Scott, who employed structural efficiency, rationalism, economy of means and geometric purity, in what could be seen as a reinvention of the traditional 'Queenslander'. For over the last three decades, Andresen O'Gorman have obsessively explored the potential of Australian hardwood timbers, and to this they bring an awareness of harmonic rhythms and mathematical proportions, which have been refined to become an ordering device. The screen has been given particular significance and becomes a filter… a filigree demarcating programmatic and spatial threshold conditions. The influence of Kerry Hill – an Australian architect working from Singapore – can be detected in many of the apparently ethereal, yet materially robust houses of this sub-tropical trajectory. His Lalu Hotel (2002) in Taiwan, and his Sunshine Beach House (2003) north of Brisbane, feature abstracted masonry forms sheathed with timber screens, and an almost classical ordering of spatial sequence. Whilst the houses by these Brisbane-based architects assert their presence with orthogonal geometries and modernist proportions, the porous and semi-transparent qualities of the walls and structure render the final object as something ephemeral and delicate.

Demonstrating a holistic engagement with sustainable place-making, the architecture of Peter Stutchbury – who first attracted attention with the fragile gemlike Israel House (1986-1992) – epitomizes this evolution of the Australian vernacular. Springwater (completed in 2006) is a monumental sculptural building, but one that still encapsulates fundamental ideas of relationship to place, and the idea of a house as a campsite. Stripped of lush and expensive finishes, this house is pared back to represent pure ideas of shelter and speaks of essential poetic dwelling. The direction taken in Stutchbury's work and in the recent houses of Alex Popov – the recurring influence of monumental modernism, the direct yet inventive treatment of materiality, and the commitment to an idea of place and landscape – is now replacing the previous Australian vernacular of corrugated-iron suspended over glass pavilions, especially in Sydney.

Contextual additions: the alteration and addition

The recent spate of alteration and addition projects by notable architects – a sign of the times, and signalling the end of the perception of Australia as the land of the free-standing house – is demonstrative of another type of architectural invention. Increasingly prevalent in an era that must consider issues of density, re-use and the preservation of historically significant precedents, these projects are subject to a complex range of regulations and difficult site conditions that are not typically found in the free-standing dwelling. Within these projects another series of thematics emerge, and *context* – whether an intact Victorian streetscape, an individual building of architectural or historical significance, or the wider context of the suburb – becomes a critical design informant. For Rex Addison, Simon Hanson, Iredale Pedersen Hook, Tonkin Zulaikha Greer and Elizabeth Watson-Brown, the fabric and materiality of the surrounding context, and their operation as a system, are integral for their processes as they work with the exigencies of a specialized project on an unlikely site. At the level of tectonics, design operations are characterized by strategies of manipulation, abstraction, extension and exaggeration. Adjacent rooflines, rhythms of openings and structure, and neighbouring materials, become reconfigured so that they speak both to the contextual surrounds and to contemporary architecture. Underpinning these formal moves, however, is a series of investigations that engage with broader issues of place-making, reuse, and sustainability. The existing house is altered to accommodate modern lifestyle, the climate and the light conditions, but also – critically – to acknowledge and to contribute to the network of surrounding urban conditions.

Two of the most startling inner-city alteration projects – Jackson Clements Burrow's Tyson Street House and James Russell's Brookes Street House – demonstrate confronting, but entirely successful solutions. Jackson Clements Burrows offer a critique of the planning and heritage regulations… instructed to take heed of the surrounding streetscape and the original Victorian façade of the house, the architects installed a 1:1 photograph of the existing façade onto an otherwise entirely contemporary piece of residential architecture. James Russell's new dwelling, a delightful timber structure, is literally grafted 'opportunistically' onto the side of a 19th century church. The eastern wall of the church thus forms one side of the first floor courtyard of the house, and the unexpected intervention also serves to activate the public forecourt area and the way in which the local community functions.

A further series of projects – Louise Nettleton's Point Piper House, the Folded House by Dale Jones-Evans, the Zulaikha Laurence House by Tonkin Zulaikha Greer with Drew Heath, the Eyelid House *(right)* by Fiona Winzar and Donovan Hill's Tibet Gallery – reveal the potential for creating beautiful contemporary dwellings within the constraints of existing buildings and sites. The central tension manifests itself as a dialogue between 'new' and 'old', and the resulting spatial narratives weave their way in and out of the 'new' and 'old'. The heavy masonry structures of the existing house typically form a counterpoint to the typically lighter timber and steel additions. Alternatively, House 42, by Dimitty Andersen in Adelaide's eastern suburbs, offers a dwelling of equal mass and weight to the existing stone house, but its planning and orientation, and its relationship with the surrounding garden, are open and flexible… in keeping with 21st century living.

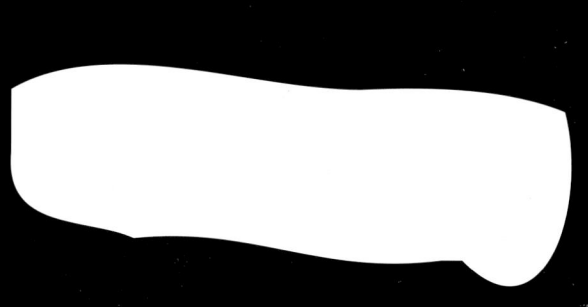

"The screw has to be turned ever further…
one has to be more violent, more avant-garde,
more abstract!"

- Sidney Nolan

The Ned Kelly series, painted by Sidney Nolan in 1946 and 1947, can be seen as one of the first local translations of early 20th century European modernism into an Australian context. One painting, simply entitled Ned Kelly, shows the defiant bushranger – black, as if there was no other colour in the world – astride a horse, riding away from the viewer towards a remote horizon. Nolan places him solid and abstract in the centre of the painting… a centaur… half man, half horse. The dry golden landscape is an expanse limited only by the horizon. The sky is blue and vibrant, with a few white clouds showing through the eye slit of Kelly's armour.

At one level, this series of paintings is a simple retelling of the events that led up to the execution of Ned Kelly in 1880: the story of an outlaw clad from head to toe in metal armour. But they are also landscape paintings. Nolan painted a coarsely executed tonal landscape, depicting an unmistakeable vision of Australia: a flat horizon, a bright sky, and the bush. Onto that landscape, Nolan placed a solid black abstraction. This dominating figure is both Ned Kelly – threatening, impenetrable, mythologized – and the pure modernist black square… half supremacist, half Picasso. The landscape is given significance through its juxtaposition with the abstraction, and this compelling image is now central to the 'idea' of Australia.

These words – which I wrote three years ago – remain relevant, if not apocryphal. Australian domestic architecture has rapidly adapted to the priorities of ameliorating our – pressing and unequivocal – environmental and social issues, and the image of Nolan's modernist abstraction stands as a potent symbol – strongly formed and boldly placed against the dry Australian landscape – of architecture's recent preoccupations.

A beautifully crafted house, formally arresting and materially rich... it possesses the informality of a holiday house and reignites post-WWII discussions of housing for an Australian context.

ARCHITECT : ASHTON RAGGATT McDOUGALL

Black, bold, yet undeniably domestic, this house appears both familiar and unfamiliar, in an almost uncanny way. Located amongst old eucalypts at the top of a rise overlooking Western Port, the house sits snugly in the sleepy Victorian coastal town of Somers. Presenting modestly to the street, the northern elevation of stained timber panelling and simple window detailing with a shallow roof-line recalls Australian beach houses of the post-WWII years. Best known for their provocative public buildings, this foray into the domestic realm challenged Ashton Raggatt McDougall's usual architectural procedures and conceptions of space. Rather than designing a project that would be – for ARM – characteristically "noisy, highly elaborated" and rife with ideology, as Ian McDougall says, this project demanded a more subtle approach, a consideration for the human scale and "for what it is to make something for someone to live in".

Rather than draw on a broad field of cultural issues and precedents, as ARM might typically do, the scope of investigation with this house is tightly focused. The Mornington Peninsula School – including the Crackers House (1951) by Osborn McCutcheon, and the Kevin Borland and Max May houses of the 1970s and early 1980s – informed the architectural language and detailing. The house does not conform to current housing trends concerned with "vanity and luxury", as Ian McDougall puts it, and the architects chose to investigate an alternative architectural lineage that has been "left behind", and this, combined with their interest in the building traditions and the "pragmatism" that characterized the 1970s houses, was the primary inspiration. McDougall recalls that ARM "wanted to dip into that thinking, see what is available, what sort of textural, sensory and yet slightly encyclopaedic historical issues could be played with, to work up a piece that would fit with the landscape and still evoke recollections of beach holidays, tearing up and down the stairs, and sliding around on the floor".

The project is more than just a stylistic emulation though: the fluid spatiality of the interior, with a faceted plywood ceiling, follows the crank in plan as the body of the house twists to accommodate existing trees. "It's a long building that has been pulled around", McDougall says, "so all the finishes and components are drawn onto that as though they were once in line, but have been dragged around. The building actually comes around in front of itself, creating its own foreground". There is an awareness of the containing object, unlike the "modernist rectangle" that simply frames the view. As McDougall observes, "it's a picturesque project", with a diversity of vanishing points rather than an authoritative singular perspective.

In the tradition of ARM's architecture over the last twenty years, the Adey House questions commonly accepted wisdoms. In this case, that includes challenging both the rural tradition as the accepted image of housing in Australian landscape – of placing objects into that landscape – and, conversely, the internationalized housing solution that has no engagement with Australian culture or climate. The result is a beautifully crafted house, formally arresting and materially rich, that possesses the informality of a holiday house and reignites post-WWII discussions of housing for an Australian context.

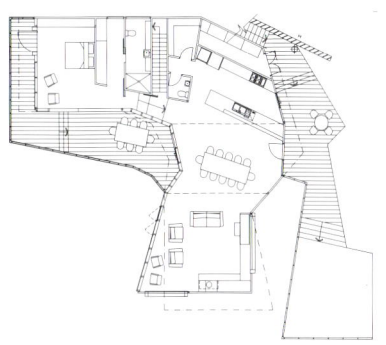
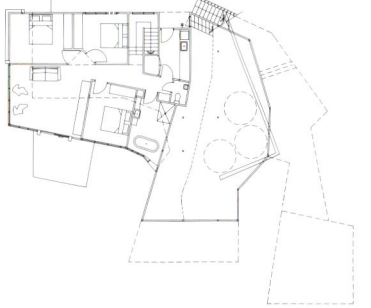

Applecross House

> The orientation of the house, with maximum exposure to the afternoon sun blazing over the western reaches of the Swan River, led to the idea that the home could be developed as an interpretation – an abstraction – of the traditional Australian veranda.

ARCHITECT : JACKSON CLEMENTS BURROWS

Set in the flat leafy landscape of the affluent suburbs south of the Swan River between Perth and Fremantle, this house – comprised of two large orthogonal pavilions – demonstrates a very specific and elemental response to the immediate physical context and the Western Australian climate. In contrast to the surrounding 'neo' villas – whose language re-erects a nostalgic (and invariably ill-conceived) idea of architectural heritage – this project is derived from a clear diagram of optimal orientation, views and cross ventilation, which is expressed in a loosely modernist arrangement of elements, materials and orthogonal geometries assembled in a clear and precise way.

The orientation of the house, with maximum exposure to the afternoon sun blazing over the western reaches of the Swan River, led to the idea that the home could be developed as an interpretation – an abstraction – of the traditional Australian veranda. The western pavilion, therefore, holds all the public living areas… configured as double-height volumes enclosed by screens of semi-transparent operable glass louvres and two tall masonry walls. The veranda has long been the place in the Australian house for informal gatherings and relaxing, and this traditional role informs the way in which the program of living spaces can work, as gatherings can occur inside, outside, or inside and outside. The expanded double-height veranda and fine timber detailing open up the interiors of the house, so that a series of spaces leading from the kitchen out to the garden can actually perform as one continuous living area. The western elevation appears from the north as a monumental transparent volume, perched on a long stone wall that leads into the house, and anchored by the two white walls at the southern end.

The eastern pavilion, which holds the kitchen, a study, bedrooms and bathrooms, is built from stone and masonry to provide thermal mass and a cooler darker environment for rest and sleep. A central circulation spine demarcates these two pavilions, defined by a honed bluestone floor that cuts through the timber flooring of the living spaces. The contrast between the mass of the eastern masonry pavilion and the lighter western 'veranda' pavilion defines the front elevation, and indeed the house itself. This language of material contrast – heavy and light, screens and walls, stone and glass – represents a recent direction in designing houses for a hot climate: an approach most closely identified with Singapore architects, such as SCDA and Bedmar & Shi. Architectural cross-pollination between Perth and Singapore could be seen as inevitable, given the (relative) adjacency of the two cities, and their ever-increasing financial and social connections. The architecture of the Applecross House is very simple and refined… directly engaging with the landscape and climate, whilst ignoring any historical affectation.

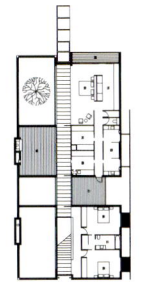

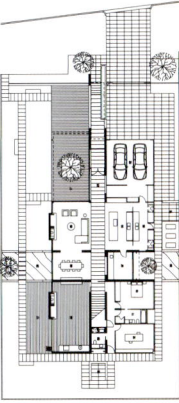

This pure composition of a scalloped concrete box floating above a recessed glazed base does not speak clearly or directly of the 'domestic', but rather reflects upon a series of ideas drawn from artists and architects alike.

ARCHITECT : WOOD MARSH

The monumental form of Wood Marsh's Barro House resides in a street of predominantly Federation houses in the Melbourne suburb of Kew. With no easily identifiable front or back, no direct relationship to its surrounds, abstract and audacious, yet undeniably handsome… this project is Wood Marsh at their best. The pure composition of a scalloped concrete box floating above a recessed glazed base does not speak clearly or directly of the 'domestic', but rather reflects upon a series of ideas drawn from artists and architects alike.

Commissioned by a client involved with the concreting industry, the brief was to 'showcase' concrete, and provide a four-bedroom house to accommodate a family and its lifestyle. The initial design developed out of the architects' material investigation, and their desire to achieve a continuous solid form that concealed joint lines. The continuous fluted external profile, which casts shadows onto adjoining surfaces, is the remarkable result. Internally, the floor is of rendered black concrete, the ceiling is grey concrete, whilst a central wall, dividing the kitchen and dining room from the living rooms, is composed of exposed aggregate. In contrast to this seemingly brutalist materiality, Wood Marsh inserted a blood-red mosaic tiled wall that runs through the living spaces and pokes out through the northern elevation. A centrally placed glass staircase leads upstairs to an equally dramatic second storey. Continuing the theme of impenetrability, all upstairs rooms are hidden behind a black stained, battened timber wall, which folds around the staircase landing. A deep circular skylight illuminates these spaces.

The concerns of Wood Marsh are not dependent on program… whether the building is a gallery or a high-rise tower, their interests lie in a layering of conceptual ideas, exploring scale, sculptural abstraction and, as they say, "the emotional life of buildings", can be pursued. "Our ambition for the architecture is that you walk away with that sense of knowing and unknowing at the same time… the buildings are not just a pragmatic solution, they are not necessarily nice or unnice [sic], beautiful or ugly". The success of their buildings is that they achieve an emotional and cerebral experience, whilst satisfying the particular requirements of the brief, and their oeuvre of completed buildings comprises robust, highly sculptural works.

Unusually, for Wood Marsh, this project makes reference to architecture rather than art. The house speaks of both Renaissance and modernist precedents, from Palladian villas to Ludwig Mies van der Rohe's and Le Corbusier's domestic projects, and the upstairs timber wall references Roy Grounds' iconic house in Hill Street, Toorak (1954). As with all Wood Marsh projects, the references are not just simple quotations, they are enveloped by their own vocabulary and architectural pursuits. The resulting architecture achieves a singular identity whilst engaging with an historical context. There are no overt ambitions to participate in discussions of an Australian architectural identity, but these architects are nonetheless carving out an unprecedented architectonic language and conceptual approach.

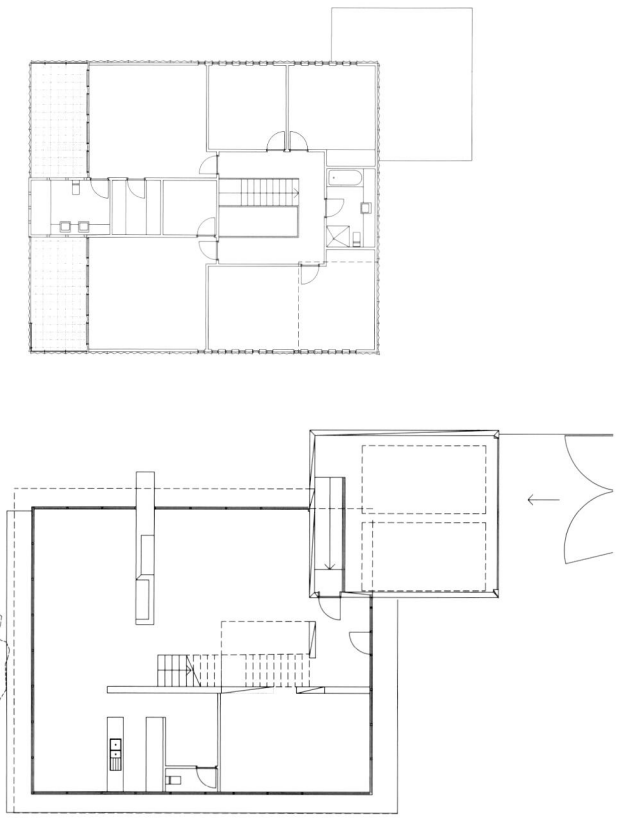

bastian farm-house

This house, with its yielding gentle relationship to its beautiful context, continues the investment that Troppo have placed into the development of an architecture that speaks directly to Australia's history and climate.

ARCHITECT : TROPPO

The Bastian Farm-house sits at the top of a hill overlooking the beautiful undulating landscape of the Clare Valley, providing the owner with uninterrupted views of his grape-growing fields below. Drawing on the longstanding tradition of the South Australian homestead – especially as seen in the Clare and Barossa Valleys – and its collection of outbuildings and sheds, the house has been fractured and separated, thus allowing the breezes and daylight to penetrate throughout the interior. Continuing Troppo's prolific output of dwellings that engage in both a literal and poetic dialogue with the landscape and environment, the plan and section of this house work to engage with its context. The plan-form engenders interactions and journeys that begin from the western approach to the site… the entrance sequence proceeds through a carefully choreographed path, with framed and considered views accompanying every transition through the interior to the ultimate panoramic view from the living room. This view looks east over a dam, which serves scenographically as a reflecting pool, both from within the house, and when looking back at the engagingly anthropomorphic forms of the house from the east. The strategy of building dispersal serves to reduce the overall bulk of the building, and provides outdoor courtyards protected from the cold southwest winter winds.

The relocation of Troppo's architecture – from its original home in the environmentally extreme conditions of the Top End to all points of Australia – has not compromised the firm's fundamental objectives. As Philip Goad observes in the firm's monograph… "A critical engagement with place, climate and culture, and how architecture might interact with and inform these issues has provided ongoing sustenance for an increasingly relevant group practice, where energy saving, the ethics of climate, and a sensitivity to landscape demand responsibility".

All the detailing and construction of the Bastian Farm-house responds to the site's environmental considerations, and the orientation maximizes the warmth of the eastern and northern sun, whilst protecting from wind and afternoon heat. Stone, timber and steel are selected and treated to recall the local vernacular traditions, and to age harmoniously and in empathy with the landscape. The slate used throughout the house was collected from the owner's grape fields, as the ploughing of the land crushes the stone and strews the pieces across the ground. Un-oiled, durable Australian hardwoods and cypress pine were used as timber, whilst the galvanized steel and zincalume sheeting are also left as natural – as unworked – as possible. This house, with its yielding gentle relationship to its beautiful context, continues the investment that Troppo have placed into the development of an architecture that speaks directly to Australia's history and climate.

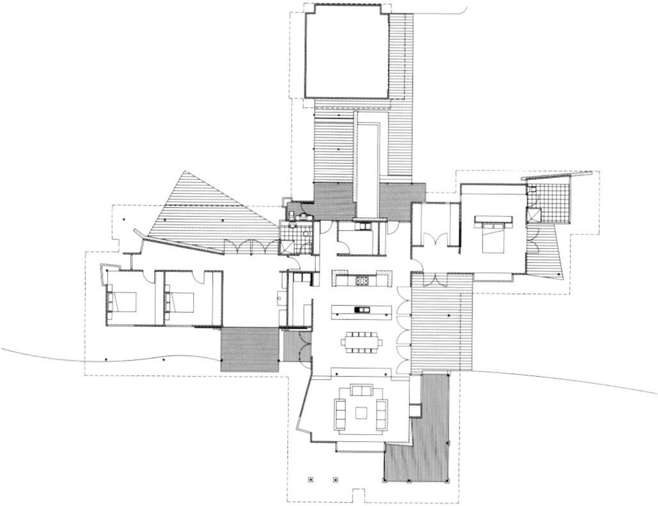

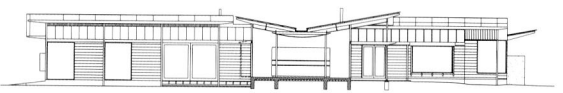

bellevue hill house

The final house of concrete, face-brick, and timber, is a highly skilled and spatially rich house that reveals this diverse and extensive architectural knowledge, but also the architects' ability to address a multiplicity of issues.

ARCHITECT : MARSH CASHMAN koolloos

At the end of the 20th century, the typology of Australia's domestic architecture underwent a major revision… one that involved both a radical rethinking of what Australian 'identity' is and what Australian 'vernacular' could be, but one that also acknowledged the last two hundred years of that architectural history. A major shift was seen… a recognition that there is no singular identity or vernacular, and that Australia is multiple by nature, inherently pluralistic in both its climate and its people. For architects now engaged in this discourse, the possibilities for valid architectural expression are endless, and this house, for a family of five in the eastern suburbs of Sydney, is a wonderful example of the potential. The client, of Lebanese heritage, brought to the process his memories of growing up in a modest, though socially interactive, house in Lebanon: one that was organized around a central living space surrounded by bedrooms. This story became central to the design process, and the plan-form of the resulting house replicates and extends that relationship of bedroom wings arranged around the living and public spaces.

Many other influences came to bear on the evolution of the house and its final three-dimensional expression. The client's professed admiration for Tadao Ando's concrete abstractions and, locally, for Hugh Buhrich's post-war houses, was incorporated into the architects' own love of 20th century modernist architects, including Rudolf Schindler and Louis Barragan, and their appreciation of recent Australian architects… diverging from the Sydney School to Durbach Block and John Wardle, to Ashton Raggatt McDougall and Peter Corrigan, and to Kerstin Thompson and Peter Stutchbury. The final house of concrete, face-brick, and timber, is a highly skilled and spatially rich house that reveals this diverse and extensive architectural knowledge, but also the architects' ability to address a multiplicity of issues.

In response to the single-storey street context, the front elevation is modest and of a comparative height. The interior space unfolds upon entry, and becomes two-storey in part, with three bedroom-wings framing a central double-height public volume. Defining that living space, the prismatic volumes of a TV room and a reading room on the first floor push back into the void. Plywood cladding, stained either a rich walnut or a solid black, wraps around these elements, as well as the ceilings and a bridge – running along the southern wall – that joins the TV and the reading room. At selected moments, bright pinks and oranges are brought into the scheme to contrast with the rawness of the materiality. Walls adjacent to the outdoor spaces are completely open-able to slide back out of view, and a large horizontal overhang shelters the interior spaces and provides a protected outdoor space. Evident in the careful material articulation of plywood and concrete, and in the folding windows and sliding doors of the public space is the influence of Shindler, and of Barragan's characteristic bold colour. This dwelling, which unites abstracted beauty, modesty and spatial diversity with clever planning, is a delightful and exemplary contemporary Australian house.

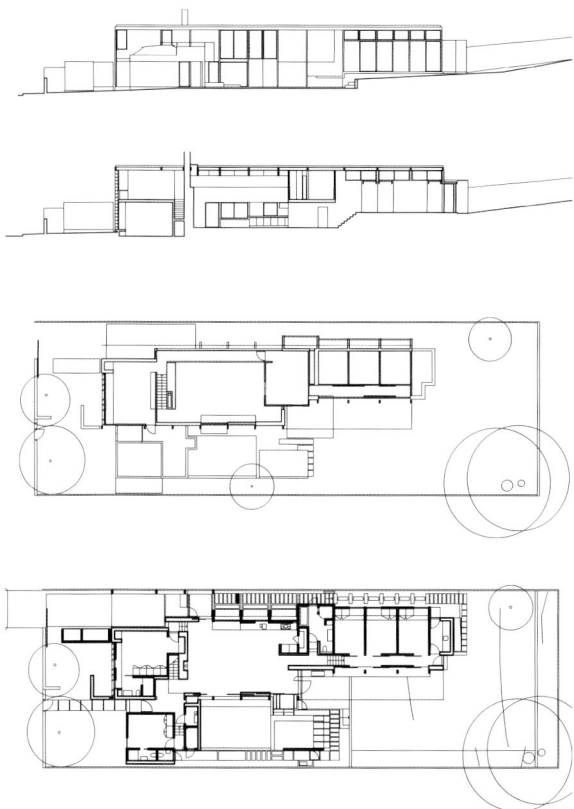

The line of the wave is used as the generating device and unifying element for this house, and its translation into an elegant refined series of forms and spaces, shifts the metaphor into a spatially sumptuous reality.

ARCHITECT : TONY OWEN NDM

This spectacular residence with a clear agenda to tease, tempt and seduce, is located one street back from Bondi Beach. The client wanted a house within which he could entertain, and one where he could feel a connection with Bondi… one which reflected the beach and the distinctive local café culture. With its white abstracted monumentalism and with an architectural language of curvilinear lines intersecting with the modernist rectangle, this house can be seen as part of a recent lineage of Sydney houses – ones showing a strong affinity with European and Scandinavian modernism – by such architects as Alex Popov, Durbach Block and, of course, Harry Seidler. However, the geometries here – metaphorically inspired by the proximity of Bondi Beach – are then given life through digital technologies. Tony Owen refers to his practice's digitally-inspired process as "elastic design", an architecture that is "pliant, yet has an inherent structure and ordering principle". The design program utilizes parametric modelling and Rhino-scripting to "create geometric relationships… which respond to environmentally specific conditions and building systems… to go down a path that is beyond imagining without a computer".

The line of the wave is used as the generating device and unifying element for this house, and its translation into an elegant refined series of forms and spaces shifts the metaphor into a spatially sumptuous reality. The line runs directly though the house, forming a southern entry wing, before rising as the ceiling above the northern living and dining areas. This ceiling curves overhead at the central staircase, at the point where upper and lower floors are literally folded into one another, and this spatiality – fluid and dynamic – is intended to be a tangible experience… spaces slip into one another and the programmatic thresholds are blurred. The phenomenon is enhanced by the materiality and the detailing, as white surfaces – sometimes stone, sometimes plaster – animate the curves when they come together and then subtly slip past one another. The ground floor is relatively solid, whilst the upper levels are more transparent, and this material treatment of masonry and glass is given emphasis through the play of light as it enters the interior.

The house (as built) will form the eastern half of the proposed final scheme, where flamboyant cantilevered extensions on the identically sized block to the west will continue the dynamic geometries. The entire project is unashamedly gestural, bestowing upon an otherwise standard-issue suburban neighbourhood of brick bungalows a sculptural connection with the adjoining world-famous beach, and (perhaps more significantly) introducing the potential of digitally-created structural geometry to Sydney's architectural tradition of abstracted modernism.

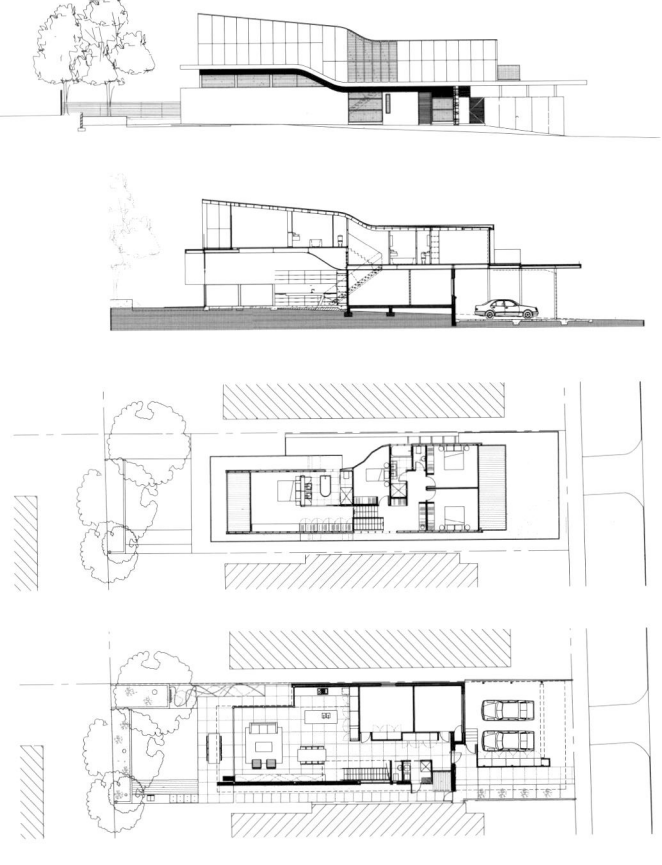

Exterior walls become a backdrop for social gatherings around the fire. Interior and exterior merge and flip, and despite its geometric purity, the house can be both a hermetically sealed container and one that unfolds... encompassing the entire site and playfully subverting the traditional pavilion type.

ARCHITECT : NEESON MURCUTT

Detached from the ground and supported by a field of hefty concrete footings, the timber-clad abstraction of the Box House neither recedes obligingly into its picturesque surrounds nor denies its rural heritage. This small abode, for an artist couple and their child, is a perfect cube measuring 6 x 6 x 6 metres. Intended as a retreat from their working lives – a "hard tent" – this project is quite a departure from the idiom of the contemporary holiday house. No gleaming white interiors or guest bedrooms here, this project has more affinity with the bush shack, the 'lean-to', or better still, the tractor shed. A timber skin wraps around three sides, whilst the fully glazed northern elevation floods the interior with daylight. Inhabitation is the event, which breaks into and transforms the project's resolute singularity. The performative qualities of the box are revealed through the simple device of timber shutters, which allow the interior to be opened up, thus letting in the elements… flies and all.

Whilst the exterior detailing achieves almost seamless elevations, the interior is much more robust. All structure – including noggings, bracing and rafters – is exposed, creating depth and plays of light and shadow. The sleeping space is on a mezzanine level, with a kitchen below and, other than a passage and shower room, the interior is one volume. A fireplace, clay oven, composting toilet and water tanks are all placed strategically around the box, extending the domestic domain. Exterior walls become a backdrop for social gatherings around the fire. Interior and exterior merge and flip, and despite its geometric purity, the house can be both a hermetically sealed container and one that unfolds… encompassing the entire site and playfully subverting the traditional pavilion type.

The design is though, more complex than it first appears. The pure cubic form reflects Nick Murcutt's expansive appreciation of the modernist idiom and, whilst Murcutt is unashamedly drawn to modernism's optimism – "the strong belief that architecture can solve problems and tackle issues front on" – he also has an intimate understanding of those 20th century buildings. A trajectory can be traced back to Rudolf Schindler's timber Studio/Residence (1921-1922) in West Hollywood, through to Le Corbusier's Le Cabanon (1952) on the Côte d'Azur, and to the houses of Louis Kahn and Steven Holl.

Murcutt – the son of Glenn Murcutt, the first Australian architect to establish an internationally known body of work that speaks of a particular idea of place – is well positioned to enter the discussions of how one might make architecture that is local, yet part of the broader architectural tradition. At the project's conception, Murcutt was well aware of that debate, and states that he wanted to avoid the "hand in glove" approach where the architecture "melds" into the landscape, thus aspiring to become at one with its context. "When I looked at Glenn's work, or Rick Leplastrier's," he explains, "what I liked about the work was as much to do with the architecture's separation and independence from the landscape. The connections to site were not necessarily as profound as the differences". The tension of the Box House then, results from the stark platonic form of the house overlaid with "the ethos of the Australian shed or shack".

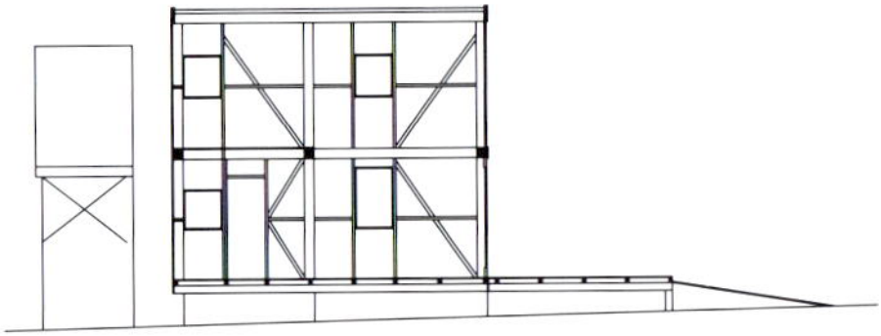

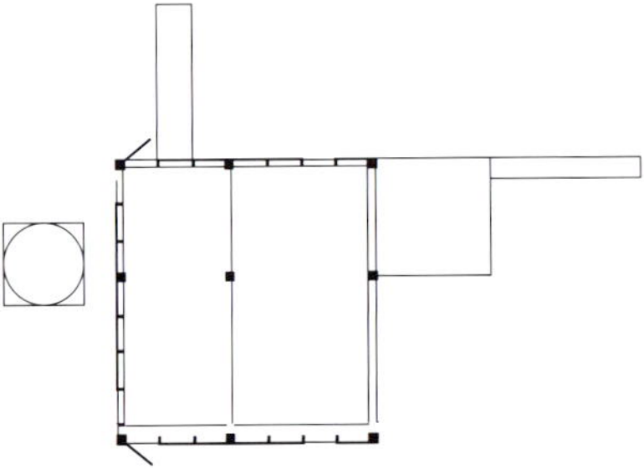

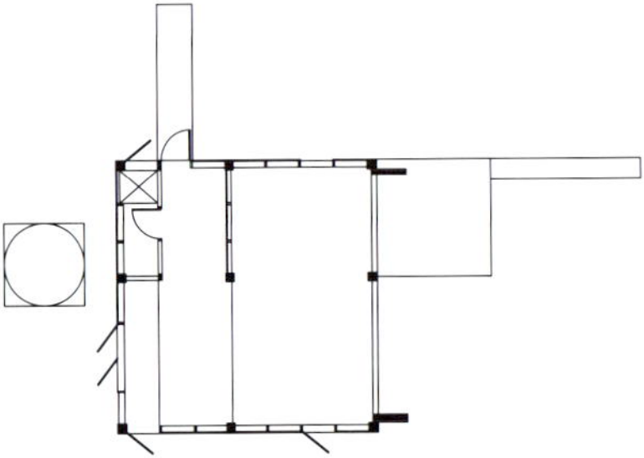

Negotiating the difficulties of building and dwelling in often contrary and fragile landscapes is an exacting challenge. This house is a tempered essay in place and in the pavilion typology, and a bold response to its dramatic location.

ARCHITECT : CRAIG ROSEVEAR

A spectacular natural landscape, dramatic views and modest desires for dwelling drive this refined house by Craig Rosevear. Located on a small headland between the Tasman Highway and Great Oyster Bay on Tasmania's east coast, with views to Schouten Island, Maria Island and the Freycinet Peninsular, this rugged land has an almost surreal, untamed sense of place. Such a beautiful and fragile setting called for great delicacy and care in the architect's approach to intervention. Anchored to the ground by a base of locally quarried stone, this steel, concrete and glass pavilion appears as a minimally enclosed platform, which defers to its surroundings and offers no formal competition or mediation by way of complex gestural forms or spatial arrangements.

The three bedroom dwelling with an open plan kitchen, dining and living area, is held tight within a long and narrow rectangular box. With the exception of a long stone wall, which runs between the carport and the house, and extends out into the landscape, the elements of the house do not intrude beyond the thin edges of the linear rectangle. The orthogonal clarity, precise steel structural system and abundant use of glass locate the house firmly within a well-established local tradition of rural place-sensitive architecture: a tradition that has its origin in the modernist pavilion typology. On this site, a desire to make the landscape experience as transparent and accessible as possible, and to do so with the least amount of disruption or mediation, finds a singular clarity of expression through a finely tempered variation upon the theme. Elemental and essential, the house is orientated towards the ocean and becomes a frame for a view.

Entry is through the stone wall and a timber courtyard, where a narrow western corridor leads past the bedrooms and bathrooms directly into the living areas and towards the view. The bedrooms and bathrooms, worked out according to Corbusian proportions and painted white, form a solid modular system within what is otherwise an entirely transparent pavilion. Seen in section, the butterfly roof lifts up and towards the horizon, heightening the momentum pushing out towards the pavilion's periphery. The living areas open up in response to the immense scale and impact of the vistas, and the finely detailed roof – tapering down to a knife-edge – suggests an architecture that prefers to recede into the background of its surroundings.

Negotiating the difficulties of building in what are often contrary and fragile landscapes is an exacting challenge, and offering a dwelling in the way of an architectural dialogue with the landscape that respects the subtlety and unforced drama of its location, whilst also providing everyday amenities, can be fraught and complex. When viewed from afar, this modest abode, measured and exacting in its execution, almost completely recedes into the landscape. A tempered essay in place and in the pavilion typology, this house is a succinct response to its dramatic location.

BROOKES STREET HOUSE

This very unusual project – literally the grafting of domestic space onto the side of a church – is a provocation, but one that results in a delightful 'cubby-house' structure suspended above the ground and embracing the surrounding context.

ARCHITECT : JAMES RUSSELL

Held, indeed squeezed, tightly between two 19th century heritage-listed buildings (one of which is a church), this house in Brisbane's Fortitude Valley provided an ideal opportunity for James Russell to explore his desire to create architecture that engages intimately with the community… stimulating exchange between the public and private realms. This very unusual project – literally the grafting of domestic space onto the side of a church – is a provocation, but one that results in a delightful 'cubby-house' structure suspended above the ground and embracing the surrounding context. Set well back from its busy street frontage, the house (for a young family) is placed literally into the shadow of the adjacent church and – in so doing – a generous leafy pedestrian forecourt is framed by the new domestic intervention and the existing public buildings.

As a raw steel and concrete-slab construction detailed with crafted timber joinery, cladding and screening, and with its various semi-industrial components and aesthetic, the building appears like a boat hoisted up in a shipyard. The ground floor entry follows a narrow staircase that leads directly into the centre of the house: an open grassed courtyard around which the program of the house is arranged. With its articulated brickwork and arched windows, the church forms the western wall of the courtyard, whose other three sides are flanked by two levels of public and private spaces. A lounge and kitchen for the adults and a play-space for the children sit at opposite ends of the courtyard, framing the sunlit grass of the outdoor zone. Bedrooms are located above each living area with a narrow bridge connecting them on the eastern edge of the house.

Climatic concerns and the need for sustainable-living are critical to Russell's architecture, and in response to the subtropical climate of Brisbane, the dwelling is entirely adjustable and adaptable. For the most part, this meant detailing the house in such a way that walls can either slide back or open up through an assemblage of timber flaps and screens. The omnipresence of the church, especially the two massive arched windows overlooking the courtyard, inspired the sparkling application of stained glass panels in the balustrading of the upper bedroom floor. This delight in ornamentation and tactile awareness reveal Russell's knowledge of craftsmanship, and the spirit of the project – engaging directly with community and with local building traditions – reflects his appreciation of the works of Geoffrey Bawa, and of the buildings of the Greek islands. This ingenious structure is a surprisingly economical and resourceful house… one which enriches both the urban context and the lives of those who live within.

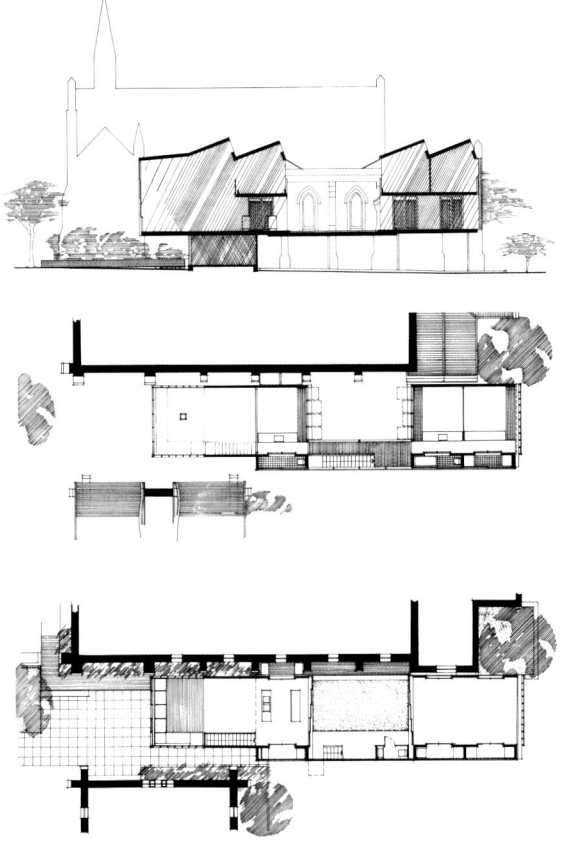

CAPE SCHANCK HOUSE

The Cape Schanck House is a witty and formally rich dwelling that challenges preconceived notions of environmentally responsive and site sensitive architecture.

ARCHITECT : PAUL MORGAN

Sustainable and environmentally responsible architecture conjures up images of a building in mimetic relationship with the surrounding context and with nature *per se:* sensitive materials, muted colours and low-key form, typically aligned to an image of iconic Australian vernacular, with timber and tin in abundance. One anticipates an architectural expression that is not too loud or sculptural, and certainly not something that looks more 'alien' than place-specific. However, Paul Morgan's Cape Schanck House – on the Mornington Peninsula southeast of Melbourne – with a conspicuous internal water tank that takes the form of a bulbous tear drop, is one house whose appearance is unexpected, and speaks of ideas that go beyond sustainability to include the physics of form… literally the kinetics of the surrounding environment and how they can create a building envelope.

From the street, this small house appears as a faceted timber and silver-metal structure. The western timber forms – which Morgan describes as a "highly sculptured and worked block" – hold the north and south entrances, three bedrooms and a bathroom, whilst the eastern aerodynamic silver form – with a distinctly 2001: A Space Odyssey profile – holds the public living spaces. Across this divide, geometries realign so that the two sides read coherently, and whilst the project fits within a contemporary genre of folded architecture, the overall expression is unexpectedly fresh, and represents the new ground being explored… that of architectural eco-morphology.

Internally, the bulging water tank orientates the living room and replaces the 'hearth' (the TV) as the centrepiece of the dwelling. Morgan wanted the ESD elements to be integrated into the project from the outset, so the design process began with a desire for an internal water tank that would function structurally, as well as environmentally. Like Morgan's contemporaneous Avalon House, the Cape Schanck House was conceived as an industrially designed object, with no separation between aesthetic and technical concerns. The architect's love of Connecticut modernism, as depicted in Ang Lee's The Ice Storm, and of the glamorous interiors of John Lautner's domestic architecture, is also evident.

The approach to site was rigorously tested through models that enacted the wind, sun and rain conditions to ensure that the design solution responded appropriately. So this 'alien' form is literally grounded in its site and responds to the specific climatic conditions. The interior, with a transparent and direct connection with the billowing tea tree landscape, and animated by the delightful sound of water running into the water tank, is soothing and otherworldly. The Cape Schanck House is a witty and formally rich dwelling that challenges preconceived notions of environmentally responsive and site-sensitive architecture.

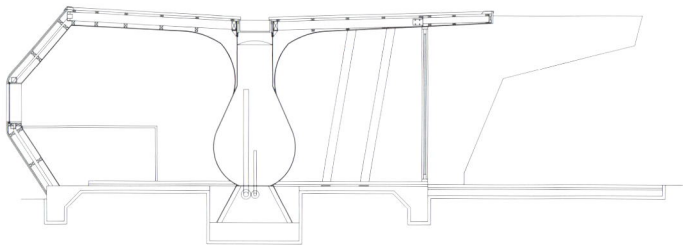

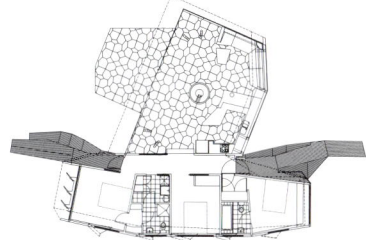

CAPE SCHANCK HOUSE AND STUDIO

Structurally, this house is an extruded cubic section stretched out to enclose simple interiors, which are animated by long cinematic views of the coast. Cruciform steel beams establish a rhythm, measuring out the dramatic seaside elevation.

ARCHITECT : denton corker marshall

Cape Schanck, at the southern tip of the Mornington Peninsula, is the spectacular location for the weekend residence and studio for Garry Emery, the renowned graphic designer and typographer. This refined elemental beach house, where roofline and wall become one, and the viewing experience is controlled, bears little resemblance to some illustrious architecturally designed neighbours, nor to their more humble fibro cousins found in coastal towns. More a sculptural intervention then a house, the building first registers as a twisted black tube floating above the native grasses and the gnarled Moonah and tea trees of the undulating dunes that surround the Cape Schanck Golf Course.

Structurally, the house is an extruded cubic section stretched out to enclose simple interiors, which are animated by long cinematic views of the coast. Cruciform steel beams establish a rhythm, measuring out the dramatic seaside elevation. Planning is refined and elegant: the dominating tube-form contains the master bedroom, the kitchen and the living areas. Materials are equally simple: raw concrete floors contrast with timber cladding, and with steel in the studio space. Between the recently completed studio and the house, a courtyard creates a spatial pause, which establishes the architectural *parti:* a dialogue between two almost identical forms.

The studio addition (completed 6 years after the original house) is an intentional copy: it takes the original's language of steel columns, glass, and twisted envelope, and simply extends it further into the landscape. Moving from the original into the void space, one is drawn into the reflected vision. As Emery says, "You experience the two simultaneously – there is reciprocity between them, one tells you about the other and vice versa". This movement between inside and outside recalls Tadao Ando's domestic work, where a spatial narrative is punctuated by outdoor spaces, and – of course – the ideas of going into and out of, and of making the architectural experience as purposely external as internal, speak of the beach house.

This house is both an exemplar of Denton Corker Marshall's polished, expressionistic architecture and the result of a collaborative friendship between Emery and John Denton that spans 30 years. Both share a love for modernism and constructivism, and have developed an intensely compositional language of precise elemental geometries, planar surfaces and refined detailing, which is all seen in the Cape Schanck House. But is it a beach house? Not really… as Denton says, "It's not a casual place, it doesn't sit comfortably with a surfboard leaning against the side. It's a bit of Garry's lifestyle moved to another location".

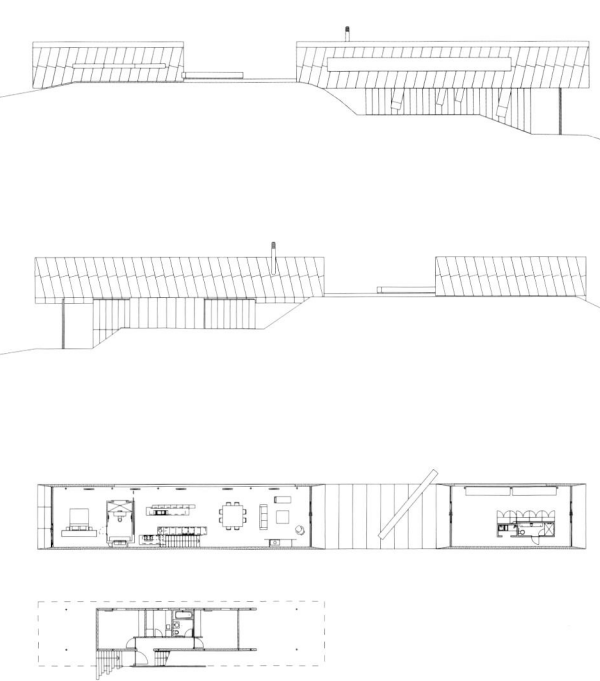

coldstream residence

This is a project whose intensity is as much psychological as it is physical: the house, stripped back to an archetypal level, gives reign for the domestic narrative to play out unpredictably across the ambiguous boundaries of its elemental enclosure.

ARCHITECT : Allan Powell

The Coldstream Residence has a rational linear concrete block form, intentionally recalling the enclaves of small industrial 'flatted' factories found in the outer suburbs of Melbourne, and the preoccupations of the house, sited on a rise overlooking vineyards and eucalypts, are not principally with the cultivated landscape it commands. Refusing expectations of the weekend retreat, the planning is not determined by the usual prerequisite framed views or grand living areas. More like an agricultural implement, or an elemental assemblage of massive walls than a domestic retreat, this project suggests archetypal memories of shelter, protection and of the spatial imagination. This is an architecture that, as Allan Powell says, is "degraded" so much that it almost melts away and suggests a more subliminal state… "what is consciously arranged seems to be very transient… it is the notion of the unfinished composition, the hint of what is implied, where reason doesn't work, and the imagination is forced to complete the work that is of interest here".

The house is configured as a long rectangle segmented by four volumes of equal proportion: the kitchen, the dining room, the living room and the master bedroom. The programmatic events are thus not dependent on planning and form, rather they are emphasized through this uniform spatial treatment. As Powell explains, "What I am trying to do is to dislocate the essential functions from the usual cultural context so they take on greater potency". Another linear concrete element sits perpendicular to the body of the house, and holds the garage and guest bedrooms. The entrance sequence moves from the garage, through a narrow timber-clad corridor into a long gallery space, and spanning almost the entire length of the house, this dark and moody gallery is profoundly arresting. Framed against the gallery, the domestic program and the experience of the other spaces always register against its presence. From other rooms one catches a glimpse of the artworks, of other goings on and, as if chasing a shadow, one is drawn into and through the house by the provocation of what lies beyond. Describing this, Powell says "You get the most incredibly potent experience by juxtaposing the highly determined and conscious against the completely unconscious. You get this fantastic frisson!"

The garage wall and the exterior elevation of the gallery define two sides of an over-scaled outdoor space, which Powell describes as a "rudimentary courtyard". A rhythm of narrow windows draws light into the gallery, and in turn, these windows frame select views of the exterior. This is an architecture where space and form are "carved out" rather than constructed, and the resulting inwardly focused project suggests an ultimately "atavistic" experience. Exterior views are encountered almost by surprise, and indeed the impact of the rather severe building form, as read against the landscape, is somewhat unexpected. This is a project whose intensity is as much psychological as it is physical: the house, stripped back to an archetypal level, gives allows the domestic narrative to play out unpredictably across the ambiguous boundaries of its elemental enclosure.

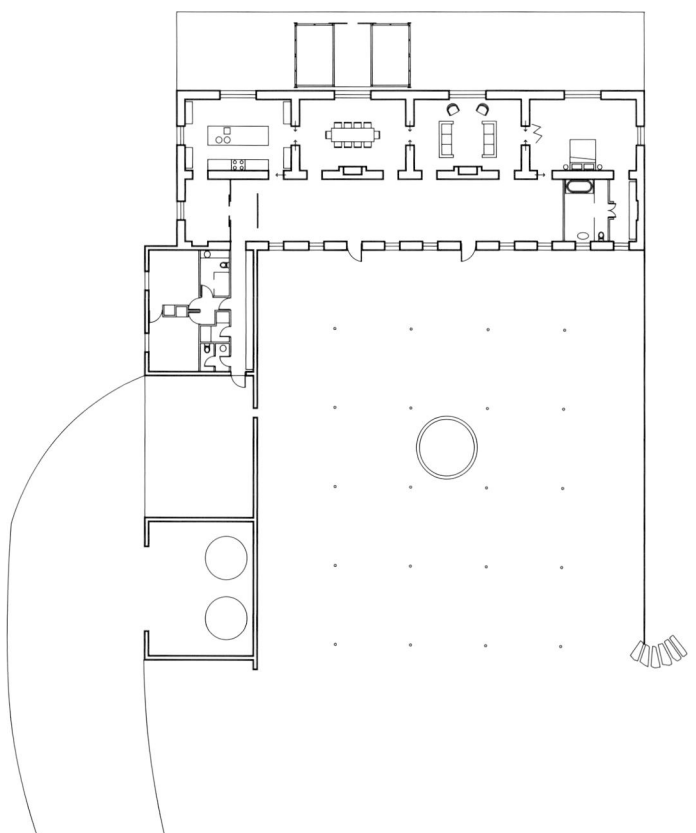

The Eyelid House is a wonderful integration of existing conditions, and an entirely new and startling design language... one that is familiar, but also provocative and unexpected in its inventiveness.

ARCHITECT : fIONA wiNZAR

The alteration and addition project, an increasingly common inner-city typology, is often a more complex design problem than the freestanding villa. Small and difficult sites, decaying existing buildings, heritage overlays, planning issues and modest budgets typically accompany these projects. Nevertheless, this type has seen some of the most inventive and satisfying architectural solutions in Australia over recent years, and the Eyelid House in Melbourne's South Yarra – with a brief to transform a constrained site with an existing single-fronted Victorian terrace into a contemporary and sustainable home for a family of five – is an excellent case in point. A hulking three-storey apartment block to the south and a three-storey motel to the east dominate the site, so in response to this, and to bring light into the interior, the roof-form was manipulated to create an 'eyelid' that screened the neighbouring giants and sheltered the rear glass façade on the east. Clad in contrasting stripes of Colorbond, the manipulated pitch of this contemporary gesture fits in with the local context of Victorian iron roof-scapes.

The geometry of the roof translates internally as a series of folded spaces, clad with tessellated plywood and translucent polycarbonate. This key design moment gives the house its unusual identity and establishes the context for an architectural language that is both expressive and contextual. This 'tension' between contemporary and traditional is continued throughout with Winzar's application of materials, which vary from raw untreated concrete, timber and steel, to the more familiar rich surfaces of stained glass, and Turkish and coloured tiles for the bathrooms and the kitchen. Scale and volume are also shifted and manipulated so that program and spatial flow are subtly suggested. Concrete shelves installed in the living room double as seating, whilst ceiling elements articulate the internal form and serve to divide the spaces.

The rear of the house was completely demolished, whilst the front three bedrooms and veranda were refurbished. Elements of the 'new' and 'fragments' of the stained glass are brought selectively into these restored areas, which retain the proportions and aesthetics of the original terrace. Continuing this stitching of 'new' and 'old', a set of sliding timber doors is used in the new main upstairs bedroom, which allow the bedroom and porch to work interactively, and hint at the interior's contemporary reworking.

Integral to Winzar's design process is a consultative briefing process, whereby the client recalls qualities and characteristics of places and buildings of importance, which then become memories and fragments… reinterpreted to give a sense of familiarity and comfort. The memory of a previous family kitchen, and of the blue and green hues of a sister's house in Byron Bay, are here intertwined into a new house in South Yarra. The Eyelid House is a wonderful integration of existing conditions, and an entirely new and startling design language… one that is familiar, but also provocative and unexpected in its inventiveness.

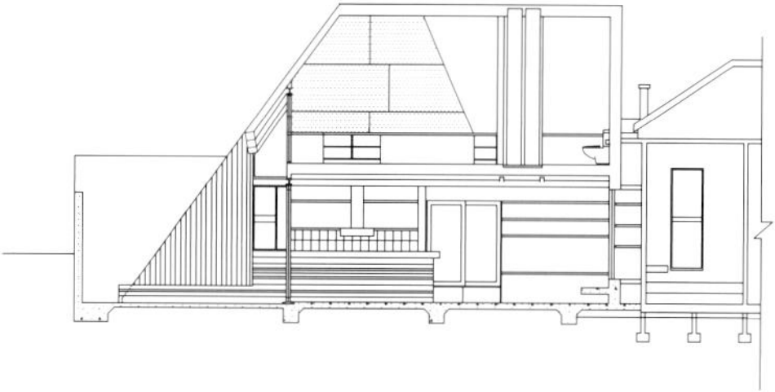

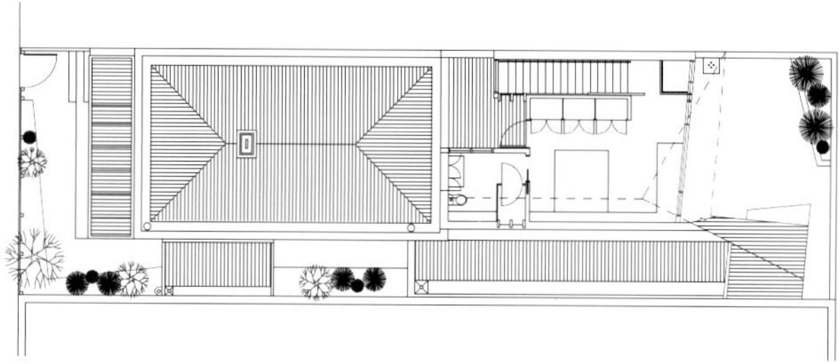

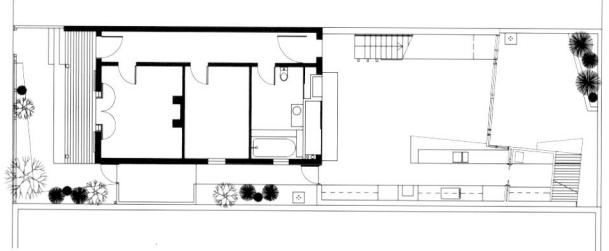

folded House

Viewed from within the interior of the 'new', the 'old' is framed and given a new emphasis, whilst looking back into the 'new', the beautiful gesture of the folded and floating copper – wrapping up over the roof and dropping back down to the ground – is brought to the fore.

ARCHITECT : dALE jONES-EVANS

An immaculately restored Victorian residence on a large site shields a contemporary 'folded' addition from the streetscape… an essay in tension and release, in 'new' contrasted with 'old', and in measured versus dynamic expression. In an unusual turn of events, the architect insisted on keeping the existing house: the interior was renovated in a "moderne" fashion and the new building – an almost separate structure – takes up the clients' additional spatial requirements. Whilst there is a seamless flow between the planning of the 'old' and the 'new', the extension's architectural language of a copper clad "origami-like" gesture, which forms a "hard shell" over the open planned modernist spaces, could hardly be more different from the existing house. The timber kitchen bench and white plasterboard ceiling of the extension take up the 'folded' theme of the exterior: curving in three dimensions, and "dripping and flowing" to form a dynamic internal space.

The transition from the existing house to the addition, and the intentional dialogue between the two, establishes the architectural *parti*. As Dale Jones-Evans says, "The new origami-like architecture emerges as a calculated placement that generates a series of interstitial inside-outside spaces, and knits together a coherent plan for a new residence". The original house contains sleeping spaces for the family, whilst the addition becomes the "living hub", configured as a series of indoor and outdoor spaces: the pool, courtyard and rear garden are separated from the dining and living rooms by full height glass sliding doors. Viewed from within the interior of the 'new', the 'old' is framed and given a new emphasis, whilst looking back in to the 'new', the beautiful gesture of the folded and floating copper – wrapping up over the roof and dropping back down to the ground – is brought to the fore. As Jones-Evans points out, the commitment to materiality and the very process of making – a sensual engagement with form and detail – can be understood as another affinity between new and old.

Aside from the restoration of the existing house, and the resolution of orientation and climate control, this project is not interested so much in a discussion about local or even regional matters, as it is with international explorations and pursuits. The folded exterior, does clearly, though not intentionally, invoke the lineage begun by Gilles Deleuze and his highly influential book 'The Fold'. Whilst the theoretical concerns of 'The Fold' are not necessarily manifest in this project and in other similar contemporary Australian houses, the book initiated a widespread international investigation known as 'Folding in Architecture', and the resulting series of buildings explored new geometries and building technologies. This house can be seen as part of this series, and its interior also recalls Preston Scott Cohen's unbuilt Torus House project, where a new torus geometry is literally pushed through an otherwise white modernist interior.

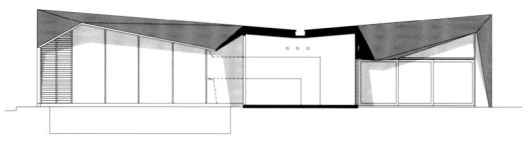

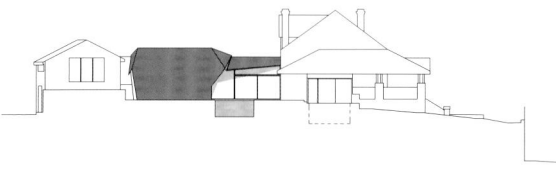

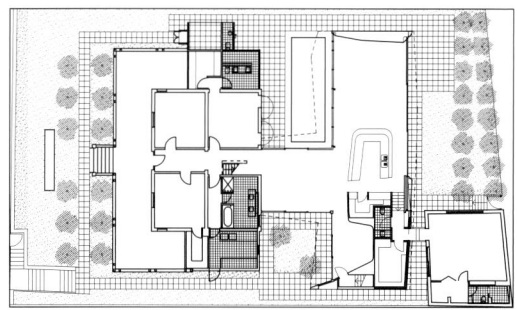

GARDEN HOUSE

> A series of interconnecting and interrelated gardens are woven through the scheme... they bleed into and merge with the pavilions, and in doing so, establish a new lifestyle that engages intimately and directly with the landscaping.

ARCHITECT : PETER STUTCHBURY

This project began in 1992 with the design of a small studio at the northern end of a suburban site in Sydney's Seaforth. The clients themselves lived in a 'project' house designed by Michael Dysart in 1977 at the southern edge of the site. Peter Stutchbury's new studio was a highly considered and precise timber pavilion, described by Philip Drew as "a small jewel-like structure, with a precise geometry of overlaid sliding diamonds". The clients' latest brief required an internal remodelling of the existing project house, along with a reconfiguration of the exterior, so that both house and studio engage completely with the connecting gardens. The existing planning was entirely transformed and simplified, with a set of pavilions inserted into the garden. A series of interconnecting and interrelated gardens are woven through the scheme... they bleed into and merge with the pavilions, and in doing so, establish a new lifestyle that engages intimately and directly with the landscaping.

This project is illustrative of Stutchbury's on-going investigation into place – *genius loci* – and the relationship between landscape and building. As with many of his houses, the notion of dwelling manifests itself as a 'glorified' and more permanent form of camping. This is achieved through flexibility of planning, and – crucially – by the establishment of a reciprocal relationship whereby the landscape and the house are equals, and in a state of continual exchange. Stutchbury's 'manner of occupation' can be seen as a series of rooms within an environment of 'micro' and 'macro' sites, which are then simply defined by a roof and not limited by walls. Here, the idea of 'house' is rethought, and a landscape has been proposed into which rooms and enclosures are placed, and when understood as a whole, become a dwelling.

The formal dining space is now a pavilion in the garden, separated from the living spaces of the remodelled house by a frangipani courtyard. Interior and exterior are in a state of constant flux, as traditional references for domesticity are challenged and replaced in a search for less permanent occupation. The existing house was reworked to flood the living areas with winter sun, and the glass doors open completely onto the gardens. Movement and social interaction flow effortlessly from one space and one program to the next, in and out of the interior and exterior spaces. The entire 'compound' feels removed from the outside world... it is connected to a deeper sense of place and of living in Australia.

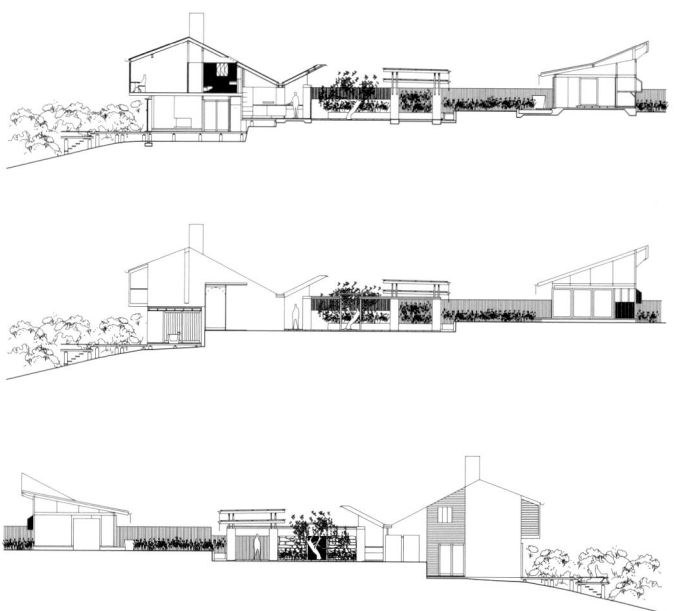

gidgegannup residence

When designing a residence in the rural landscape of Gidgegannup, 40 kilometres northeast of Perth, Iredale Pedersen Hook aimed to avoid any cliché… they conceived of a dwelling that would simply and economically engage with the physicality of the surrounding landscape.

architect : iredale pederson hook

To build appropriately and sensitively in the Australian countryside has perhaps become a loaded endeavour, as a consequence of the architecture of Glenn Murcutt: Australia's most recognized and internationally respected (Pritzker Prize winning) practitioner. Murcutt's work draws on a particular history of indigenous architecture – albeit tempered by the European modernism of Mies Van der Rohe – and, when accompanied by the rhetorical catchphrase of 'touching the earth lightly', has had both a constraining and a contentious impact on issues of relevant and meaningful identity in Australian architecture. When designing a residence in the rural landscape of Gidgegannup, 40 kilometres northeast of Perth, Iredale Pedersen Hook aimed to avoid any cliché… they conceived of a dwelling that would simply and economically engage with the physicality of the surrounding landscape.

The result is an elegant building, which relates to its rugged, defiantly Australian location – intimately and from a distance – and reflects the local vernacular of utilitarian farming buildings, whose bright linear forms become a datum within the landscape: a line between ground and sky. Located between a large body of native trees on the property's western edge and a mature eucalypt to the east, the house veers – on a 'boomerang' plan – from an initial elevation of 300mm at the northwest to a 5.5m cantilever at its eastern end. Viewed from above, the house hovers above the vista of distant hills and valleys, with two wings pivoting from the entry vestibule. The northwest wing contains the children's bedrooms and a TV room, whilst the eastern wing comprises the open living and dining areas, with the parents' bedroom at the end, above an office and carport. A timber deck and swimming pool project out into the landscape to the north, on axis with the entry and bisecting the 'boomerang' plan. Resembling a large water tank attached to a local farmhouse, a music room sits at the rear of the house, whilst all the other rooms – strung along the length of the house – are open to the views across the broad valley. The bedrooms in the northwest wing are connected by a rear corridor, which – clad in translucent polycarbonate cladding – looks out to the trees above the house on the west.

With its very elemental geometries and economic treatment of windows and detailing, the Gidgegannup Residence is a deceptively simple and familiar country house, unremarkably clad in corrugated iron. However, this economy of gesture and planning reveals architectural ideas – and an expression – of dexterity and resolve.

THE GREAT WALL OF WARBURTON

For BKK Architects, a practice equally engaged with the conceptual potential of architecture as they are with the reality of building and construction, this house at Warburton, northeast of Melbourne, is a powerful example of an architecture that is rich: both poetically and in terms of its tectonic resolution.

ARCHITECT : bkk

To mark the ground, or alternatively, to mark paper, is to suggest threshold: a demarcation of one kind or another. The line is also the beginning of form, the suggestion of enclosure, and thus protection and retreat. For BKK Architects, a practice equally engaged with the conceptual potential of architecture as they are with the reality of building and construction, this house at Warburton, northeast of Melbourne, is a powerful example of an architecture that is rich: both poetically and in terms of its tectonic resolution. It is the very act of building – of placing a wall into the Australian landscape and what that suggests for space and form – that is of concern here. Taking other rural houses by Melbourne-based architects as precedents, such as the Marshall House (1995) and Sheep Farm House (1999) by Denton Corker Marshall, and Kerstin Thompson's House at Lake Connewarre (2002), this residence explores that relentless potential of the wall. This 'Great Wall' of Warburton is expanded to be occupiable… an inhabitable threshold stretched to follow the view, and gently twisted to enclose space.

Set on an elevated site, with its timber-clad northern façade clearly visible from afar, the house withholds itself upon approach from the south, where it appears as a mute concrete wall embedded into the site. This demeanour is given emphasis through the materiality of that primary gesture, which secures the project back into the landscape and which delays the experience of the magnificent bucolic panoramic views until the house is entered. The wall is a counterpoint to the rest of the glass and timber building, which is, in reality, a light-filled pavilion.

Once past the compressed entry, at the pivot of the dogleg plan, the experience explodes into the views, with the twists of the circulation corridor modulating that visual journey. The programmatic dispersal of bedrooms, living and dining areas, and the kitchen and bathrooms, remains essentially one room wide, with the narrow circulation corridor strung out behind. Each interior space thus becomes a framing device, subtly differentiating the outlook. A material palette of rich warm timber continues beyond the fenestration line, and this external extension of the interior contributes to a sense of immersion within the landscape. The large timber deck – featuring geometric ponds, pools and a spa-bath – is a fabulous stage for basking in the morning sun and gazing across the farmlands and mountains of the upper Yarra Valley. This house is a place for retreat and transformation… one enters an almost otherworldly environment.

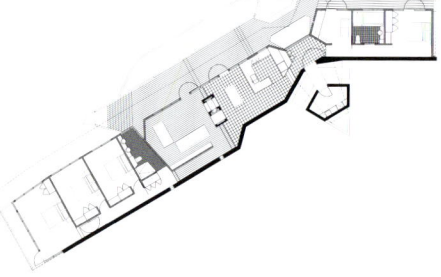

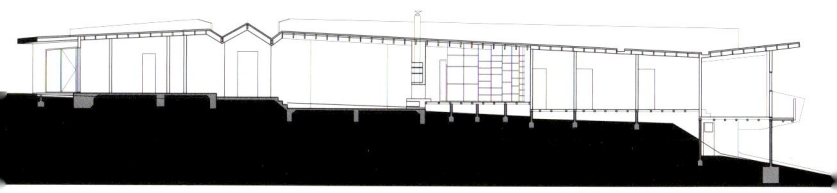

HIGHGATE HILL RESIDENCE

The Highgate Hill Residence continues a thread of South East Queensland projects that offer valid alternatives to the Queensland domestic vernacular... a thread which has become an architectural progression in its own right.

ARCHITECT : RICHARD KIRK

Perched to the east of a ravine running south from Dornoch Terrace, one of Brisbane's oldest ridgeline roads, the Highgate Hill Residence is an elegant example of climatically responsive contemporary modernism. Richard Kirk Architects – following on from the well-publicized recent houses by Australian architects Andresen O'Gorman, Kerry Hill and Sean Godsell – explore clean orthogonal geometries articulated by finely crafted timber screens and cladding systems. The nearby Rosebery House (1998) by Andresen O'Gorman can be seen as an entire screen-as-house, whilst the Ogilvie House (2003) by Kerry Hill at Sunshine Beach, north of Brisbane, is characterized by a choreographed spatial progression through forms clad at their edge by timber screens. These recent Southeast Queensland houses, as well as some by Donovan Hill, suggest the existence of a distinct local strategy, but the Highgate Hill Residence also pays homage to the modernist houses designed by Hayes and Scott in 1950s Brisbane, which were in turn influenced by Breuer, Niemeyer and Gropius. The Highgate Residence's profile of a butterfly roof atop a wall of vertical timber strips can also be seen, albeit in a much simpler form, in the Graham House (1959) by Hayes and Scott in Indooroopilly: a house which also betrays the influences of Harry Seidler's 1950s Sydney houses.

Internally, the spaces are highly choreographed responses to the various requirements for flexible engagement with the outdoors, for social gatherings and for privacy. Sited on a steeply sloping block with an existing lush and mature landscape, this five-bedroom house for a young family has been designed with two distinct identities – to the north and east, and to the south and west – that respond alternatively to the conditions and the context. On the northern side, where the site drops away into the landscape, the façade of the house breaks down into a series of moments and openings that embrace the landscape, whilst on the eastern street elevation, the building presents as a more diminutive veiled series of elements. All timbers were selected for their weathering qualities and for the manner in which they will alter and change, given their particular orientation and placement. The significant size of the house on such a steep slope and its relationship to the distant views can be seen on the western and southern elevations, but the monumentality is softened by timber battens and detailing.

The rectangular form of the building is arranged over three levels with living and dining spaces on the middle entry level, which integrates with the gardens and the swimming pool to become one luxurious indoor-outdoor space. All bedrooms are located on the upper level, whilst the lower floor holds a guest bedroom and media spaces. The internal void space, glazed on the northern side, operates in two ways: as a spatial response to the tall trees on the north of the site, and to separate the children's bedrooms from the parents'. Uniting all three floors, the staircase becomes a sculptural element in its own right, and works as an organizational reference between the levels. The Highgate Hill Residence continues a thread of South East Queensland projects that offer tangible alternatives to the Queensland domestic vernacular… a thread which has become an architectural progression in its own right.

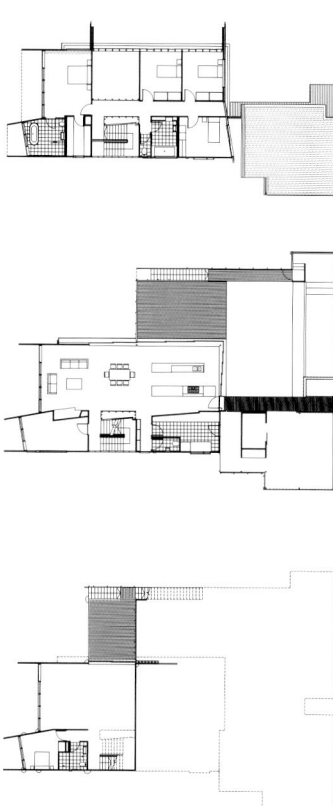

Perched on the precipice of a cliff with panoramic ocean views, this house is a series of expressionist forms strung out along the length of its site, with each element offering a distinctive experience.

ARCHITECT : durbach block

Dover Heights, an unremarkable eastern Sydney suburb of quarter acre plots ending abruptly at a cliff edge, is the context for this entirely remarkable house by Durbach Block. With its soaring white cantilever and spatial acrobatics, the project displays an unusual architectural sophistication. Perched on the precipice of a cliff with panoramic ocean views, the house is a series of expressionist forms strung out along the length of its site, with each element offering a distinctive experience. A series of elastic curves, each with their own radii and trajectories, describe the plan. Read in contrast to the contours of site, these lines generate a plan-form of unusual beauty, recalling those same loose geometries found in a Picasso painting, or, as was intended, in the Casa Ugalde, Barcelona (1951), by José Antonio Coderch. In particular, it was, as Neil Durbach passionately explains, the "mad complexity that Coderch achieved, where the inside and outside were in an incredibly fluid, interlocked kind of relationship", that they were aiming for with this house.

As with Durbach Block's Spry House (built in the same year), the first view of this project conceals the internal spatial gymnastics and unfolding drama. Beyond the humble entry and modest timber garage, a curving line encircling the kitchen leads deep into the house's centre. From this position one can best understand the cantilevered bodies of the two primary living spaces with their gently curving walls and framed views. Durbach describes the difficulty of designing for Sydney sites with such spectacular views: "It's a real problem, the stranglehold the view has over Sydney, and the risk that it can lead to an incredibly monotonous relationship". The architects looked to Jørn Utzon's own house in Porto Petro, Mallorca (1972), which used deep windows to "particularize" the views... "We made these huge bay windows. One looking south deals with the incredible storms, and the other north-facing window is totally openable and makes the room almost an exterior space".

From that same central vantage point one can also enter an open circular courtyard, which provides another living alternative. Following a staircase leading down and away from the courtyard, one feels somewhat removed from Australia. The sea views, the cliff edge and the solid white walls recall experiences of the Mediterranean coast. The lower level of the building is tucked securely into the cliff and, with its stone detailing, gives the project a certain *gravitas*. At the end of the path, a pool appears to float effortlessly out to sea.

The architecture of this house, whilst almost studiously site-specific, has an architectonic language that speaks directly to European models and indeed European Modernism. As Coderch himself said, "It isn't genius we need right now... but a truly alive building"... and that is what the Holman House offers.

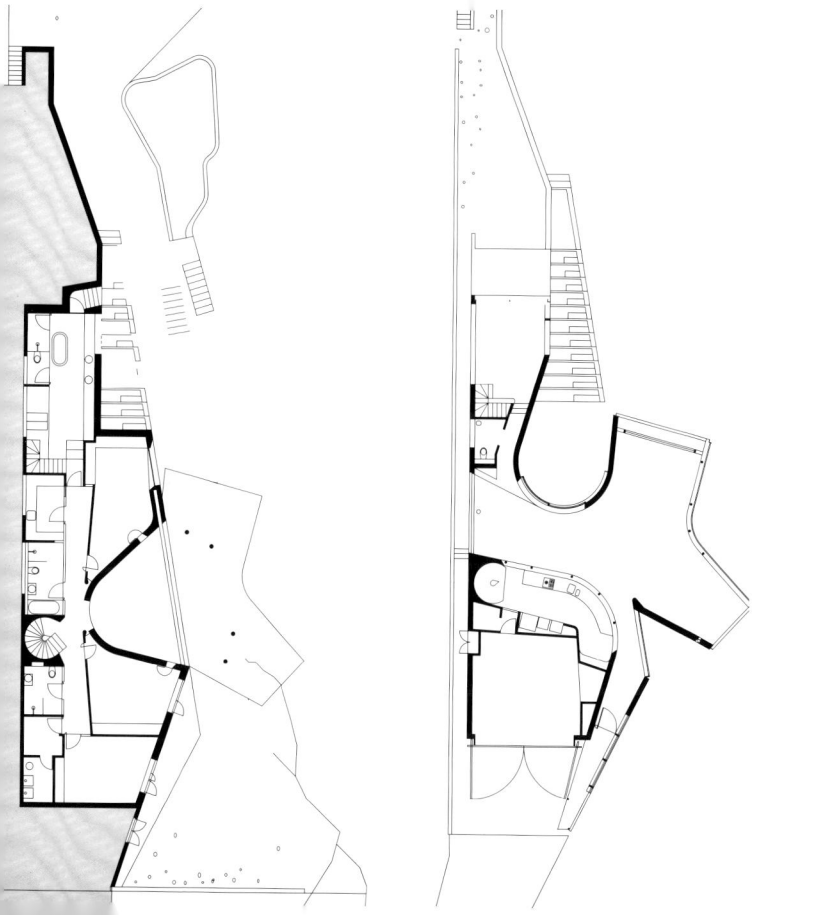

House 42, a white cubic addition to an old sandstone dwelling, adopts the abstracted orthogonal geometries, masonry and stone construction of the Spanish model, tempered by timber detailing, open planning and a fluid transition from inside to outside.

ARCHITECT : dimitty ANdERSEN

For over 200 years, and through all its variations, the evolution of Australian domestic architecture has had a longstanding relationship with Spanish architecture. With obvious similarities in the climate, the light and (to some extent) the lifestyle, Australian architects have looked to Spanish architecture as a precedent and for inspiration. From the traditional white stuccoed Spanish villas to the works of Spanish modernists, such as José Coderch, and most recently to the contemporary minimalists, such as Alberto Campo Baeza, Spanish models have been transported and modified, and used as inspiration for an Australian expression at odds with the more easily identifiable lightweight typology. Many of Alex Popov's recent housing projects – the Canopy Apartments (Cammeray, Sydney, 2004) and the Northbridge House (Sydney, 2003) – have clearly utilized the Spanish predilection for white walls, clean lines and unambiguous open space: an architecture clearly appropriate for Australian living. As with Popov, other Australian architects, such as Harry Seidler, Durbach Block and Donovan Hill have integrated a Spanish (and a Scandinavian) sensitivity into many of their most assured domestic projects.

House 42, a white cubic addition to an old sandstone dwelling (dating from the first decade of the 20th century) set well back in its own grounds in the eastern suburbs of Adelaide, adopts the abstracted orthogonal geometries, masonry and stone construction of the Spanish model, tempered by timber detailing, open planning and a fluid transition from inside to outside. The existing dark internalized house now extends into a flexible living space, which is completely open to the gardens, a tennis court and swimming pool. Andersen avoids any obvious dialogue between the 'new' and the 'old', other than the insertion of a large sandstone volume – external barbeque and internal fireplace – into the western glass wall of the extension. Subtle connections are, though, established through planning and through the use of masonry, which continues the monumentality of the older house. To emphasize the intentionally contrasting relationship between the house and the extension, the entry point is now located between the two structures, with a sedate – almost classical – vestibule.

From the surrounding gardens, the extension appears as an abstracted prismatic volume into which expansive cuts have been made… transparently exposing the interior to the landscape. The simplicity of the formal gesture – both in its solidity and its transparency, and with its contrasts of solid and void, and expansion and compression – has provided an assured and robust architectural statement… a singular and unexpected complement to the existing house.

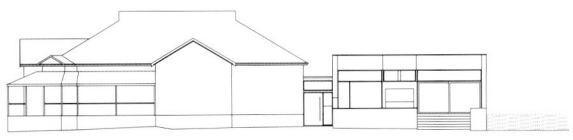

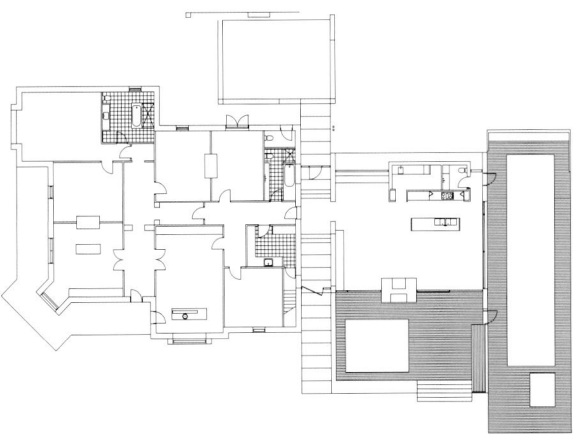

HOUSE OF ORANGE

The approach to the House of Orange – on a sloping site in Brisbane's inner northeastern suburb of Clayfield – was to work carefully with an existing house... modifying, adapting and extending the building, rather than demolishing and starting from scratch.

ARCHITECT : ELIZABETH WATSON-BROWN

For Elizabeth Watson-Brown, sustainability is as much concerned with the conservation and reuse of existing built fabric as it is with new technologies applied to new buildings. For Watson-Brown, the vocabulary of the architect needs to include such terms as 'modesty', 'ethics' and 'responsibility'... not just material, form and space. The approach to the House of Orange – on a sloping site in Brisbane's inner northeastern suburb of Clayfield – was to work carefully with an existing house... modifying, adapting and extending the building, rather than demolishing and starting from scratch. As Watson-Brown states, "Architects have a responsibility to engage and retain the quality and character of fragile inner-residential zones," and by doing so with the House of Orange, the character of the existing house was retained and enhanced.

From the street, only the existing building – an original timber 'Queenslander' – is evident, but upon entry through the centrally located hall, the spaces open out to the rear of the house and the north-facing landscape beyond. The proportions and scale of the original house – particularly the individual rooms – inform the proportions and geometries of the addition to become the building blocks and the units of the 'new'. In a similar strategy, the existing axes, rhythms and view-lines were extended into the addition, deferring to the old house whilst creating a harmonious whole. Programmatically, the addition holds new living areas of both intimate and expansive scales, a new master bedroom, an outdoor dining area, and a swimming pool and deck that extend over the gardens. Once through the transition from 'old' to 'new', the architectural language shifts beyond the original's vernacular to an entirely contemporary and modern structure of orthogonal geometries, and to assemblages of timber screens, cladding and pathways. The prospect and the climatic advantages of the site are fully revealed... sunlight floods the warm timber tones of the new spaces, creating an overwhelming orange glow and – in conjunction with the views over the magnificent northern garden – establishing a blissful Arcadian ambience.

Watson-Brown continued the original cottage's palette of materials, but altered and reconfigured the manner in which they were applied and detailed. Environmental sustainability plays out in the planning and zoning of the house, resulting in a house with an entirely passive climatic design (no air-conditioning) and one that, importantly, retains the character and environment of the existing building and site. The footprint of the original has only been minimally increased... in accordance with the architect's desire for a "carefully calibrated and modestly scaled addition".

> This modest dwelling, like much of Thompson's work, achieves a planning that is intimate, protective and tranquil... sheltered by a formally supple and geometrically expressive building.

ARCHITECT : KERSTIN THOMPSON

Kerstin Thompson Architects is one of the rare Australian practices whose work successfully engages architectural discourse – theory and concepts – with the exploration of particular ideas of form, space and dwelling. The Ivanhoe House continues ideas and ambitions beautifully expressed in the House at Lake Connewarre (2002), which included a specific response to local site conditions and the poetic possibilities of building within that context, and a resolution of the very tectonic issues of manipulating the roof plane, idiosyncratic interior volumes and highly differentiated spaces within a material palette of timber construction and black timber cladding.

An expansive Australian farming landscape is the context for the House at Lake Connewarre, whilst the local historical context of a Melbourne suburb is the informant for this latest house. Ivanhoe is home for the iconic explorations of Harold Desbrowe-Annear, and in particular, his three Chadwick houses (1903) in the small enclave of Eaglemont overlooking the Yarra River. The potential of the Arts and Crafts movement for Melbourne was dynamically explored in these houses, and they form a fundamental reference for Thompson's house… the project is both a homage to and an extension of Desbrowe-Annear and his ideas. Visually this is evident in a number of ways, most notably a taut black timber skin contrasting with natural timber louvres, and exterior 'bulges' and folds that correspond directly with the internal program. The spirit of Desbrowe-Annear is also present in the internal sculpting of space, which is modulated and modelled in response to the various programs of domesticity and to the exterior views. Built-in furniture, window seating and flexible wall details continue the legacy, although these features are also characteristic of Thompson's work.

The house is not simply an adulatory essay on Desbrowe-Annear… it is reflective of a contemporary architect preoccupied by architectural knowledge, and specifically the history of Melbourne architecture. The expressiveness of the plan-form, and the use of split corridors and angled geometries, reveal Thompson's interest in the work of Edmond and Corrigan – especially the Athan House (1988) – whereas the looseness and informality of space recalls Robinson Chen's Hildebrand House (1990) and the work of Kevin Borland. Comprising a linear sequential organization of space, the Ivanhoe House forms a roughly squarish plan enclosing a courtyard, and this exploration of continuous space with an internal courtyard recalls the Grounds House in Hill Street, Toorak (1954) by Roy Grounds. In response to Ivanhoe's flood-plain level, the house is raised 4 metres above ground, which allows for a dramatic entrance under and then up into the centre of the home. This modest dwelling, like much of Thompson's work, achieves a planning that is intimate, protective and tranquil… sheltered by a formally supple and geometrically expressive building.

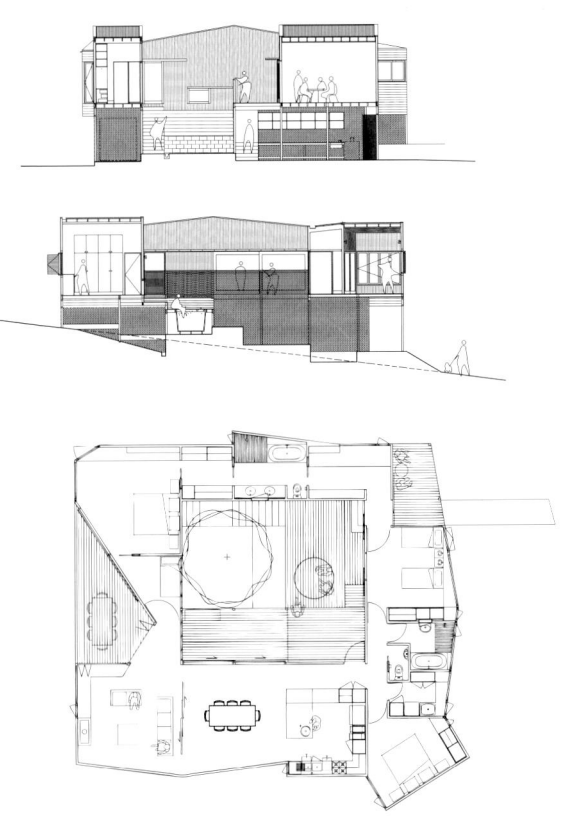

JAMES ROBERTSON HOUSE

Usually, 'public' and 'private' merge and intertwine within the domestic realm, but here an explicit physical separation is established… one that also has a psychological dimension.

ARCHITECT : CASEY BROWN

Enclosed, more solid than transparent, a singular 'whole' is how we might typically imagine the 'home'… a private, protective retreat. It is these ideas of the house that Casey Brown challenge in their James Robertson House. Located on a precarious site overlooking Pittwater, with a 40-degree slope and uninterrupted views, the 'house' is comprised of two detached glass pavilions, one perched above the other, and separated by a considerable gap of 25 metres. Usually, 'public' and 'private' merge and intertwine within the domestic realm, but here an explicit physical separation is established… one that also has a psychological dimension. The higher of the two pavilions contains the master bedroom and bathroom, whilst the lower two-storey pavilion contains the living area, the kitchen and the dining room on the upper floor, with a study and spare bedroom below. An inclinator scales the steep slope between the two pavilions.

The architects describe the entrance as "nebulous": a winding pathway leads off the beach and up into the sandstone 'plinth' base of the lower pavilion; stairs along the side of the house lead to a timber pathway tucked between the cliff-face and the living room; and turning again, the journey finally ends in another transitional zone – a spatial pause – linking the dining and living spaces.

In response to the outlook and to the temperate climate, the house is constructed from a lightweight steel system, which supports the glass pavilions and a series of outdoor spaces. The breeze blows through the interior, bringing with it the scent of seawater and the surrounding eucalypt bushland. Assembled like fallen leaves, a series of overlapping, yet detached, corrugated copper roof planes shelter and shade the decks and the fully glazed rooms. The framing system of black columns gives definition to the otherwise transparent spaces, and simultaneously frames the landscape beyond, connecting the architecture back to the dark tones of the surrounding bush.

At first glance, the house could be wrongly assessed as another project framing spectacular views and adopting a familiar Australian bush vernacular. True, with its corrugated skillion roofs, the house recalls a formal vocabulary particular to the local architectural heritage, including the works of Glenn Murcutt and Richard Leplastrier. However, a critical element of this house reflects the architects' intensive training in England, working in the guild tradition on heritage buildings, which nurtured a respect for architectural construction and materiality, and for the art of making buildings. Circulation through the project, weaving a sensual journey through and around both exterior and interior, is inspired by Japanese architecture and traditional notions of the 'village', where the experience is as much about moving between buildings and through the site as it is about being in the house itself. This is a relatively modest house, artfully sculpted into its site in such a way that one's experience of the site and of what it is to 'dwell' is thoroughly enhanced.

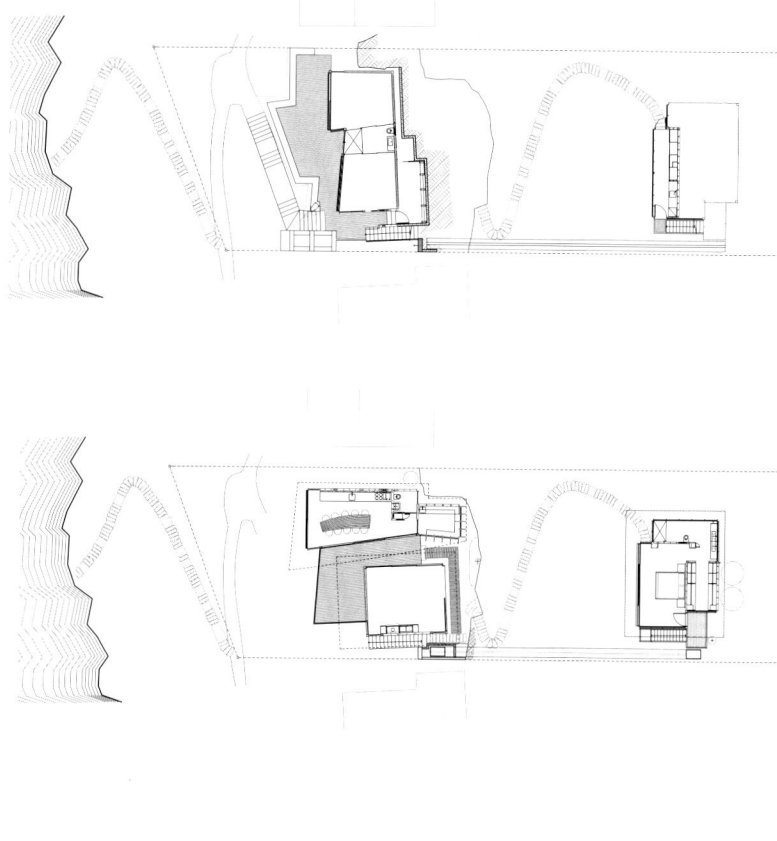

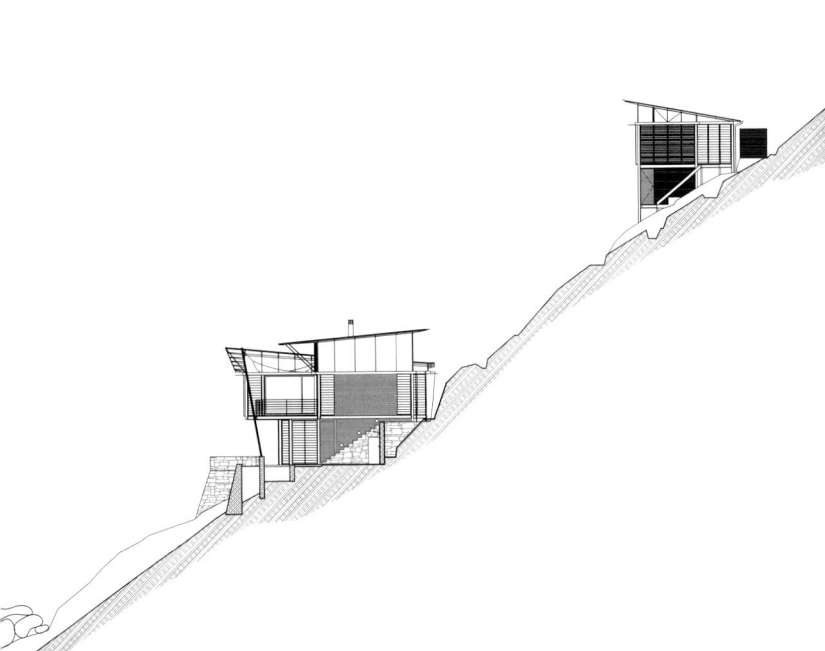

KLEIN BOTTLE HOUSE

Architecturally, spatial relationships and configurations can potentially expand beyond traditional orthogonal Cartesian models of architectural representation and construction, and the Klein Bottle House has an extreme (though playful) beauty and elegance.

ARCHITECT : McBride Charles Ryan

Buried within the dense tea treed landscape of the Mornington Peninsula, southeast of Melbourne, the Klein Bottle House responds to contemporary international investigations of topological mathematics and their translation into architecture, as well as referencing the Melbourne geometric experiments of the 1950s, as seen in the houses of Peter McIntyre, Robin Boyd and Roy Grounds, amongst others. The conceptual plurality and highly abstracted formal arrangement of the project extends McBride Charles Ryan's investigation of alternative processors of architectural formation and representation, as well as providing the very simple requirements of a holiday house… thus evoking memories of lightweight beach houses with spatial journeys that lead through and into landscape.

Three bedrooms, a rumpus room, and a large living and dining space are configured in a faceted spiral with a regal staircase that works its way around a central intimate courtyard. This primary gesture of the spiral emerged from the architects' investigation into the 'Klein Bottle': a descriptive (formal) model of continuous surfaces that remain topologically intact despite any manipulations or distortions made to its construction. Architecturally, spatial relationships and configurations can potentially expand beyond traditional orthogonal Cartesian models of architectural representation and construction, and the Klein Bottle House has an extreme (though playful) beauty and elegance. Folded fibre-cement planes and angled surfaces – rendered in greys, deep olives and white – yield and shift in response to the sea of surrounding tea trees.

McBride Charles Ryan have orchestrated a contrasting, and almost confounding, relationship between landscape and architecture: the highly contemporary architectonics of the building seem almost unreal – a *simulacrum* – not quite present. This plasticity of form emerges also from an interest in the entropic potential of representation and final outcome to collapse, and to become interchangeable. And, as with Denton Corker Marshall's Cape Schanck House and Studio (1999-2005), and Paul Morgan's Cape Schanck House (2006) – both nearby and surrounded by tea trees – the experience of the building is of juxtaposition, and of something slightly foreign. And yet, from afar, the folded twisting planes and surfaces simply register as further undulations and variations within a rugged terrain.

Internally, the external language continues, but the architects continue their love of colour and warm materials, applying a bold palette of clown-red for the staircase carpet and walls. Pale timbers are used for the living room floors, in contrast with the almost black joinery and with the bright white ceilings and bench tops. The angled walls juxtaposed with the suppleness of the twisted tea trees offer a spectacular vision, protecting the womb-like interior from the dramatic landscape and climate… and, alternatively, revealing its beauty.

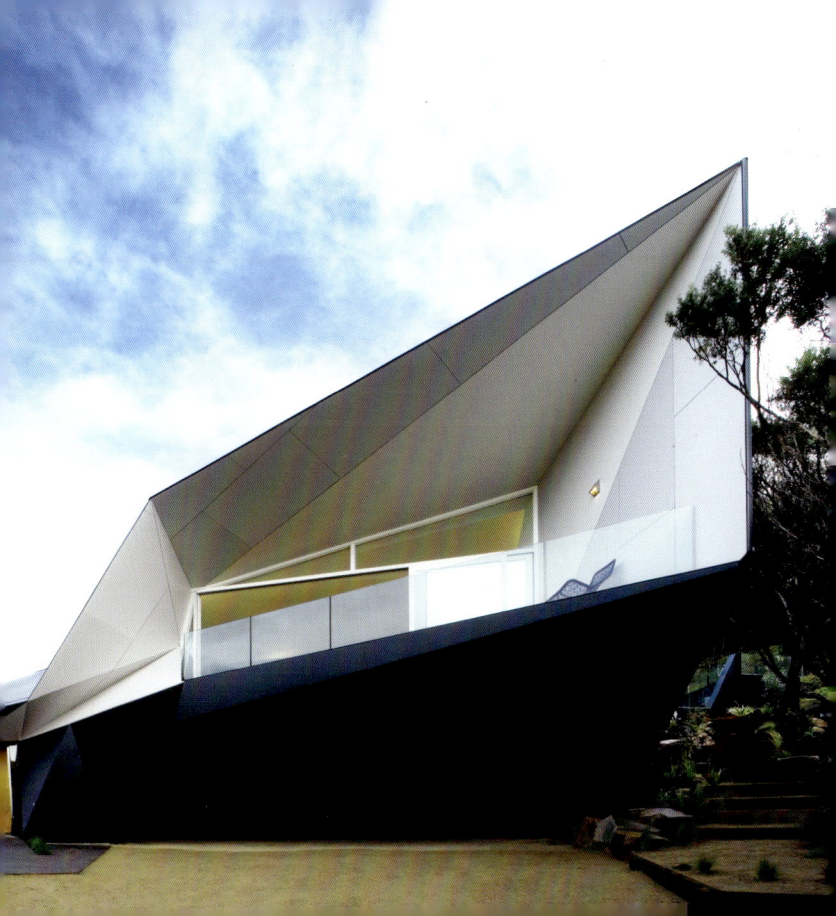

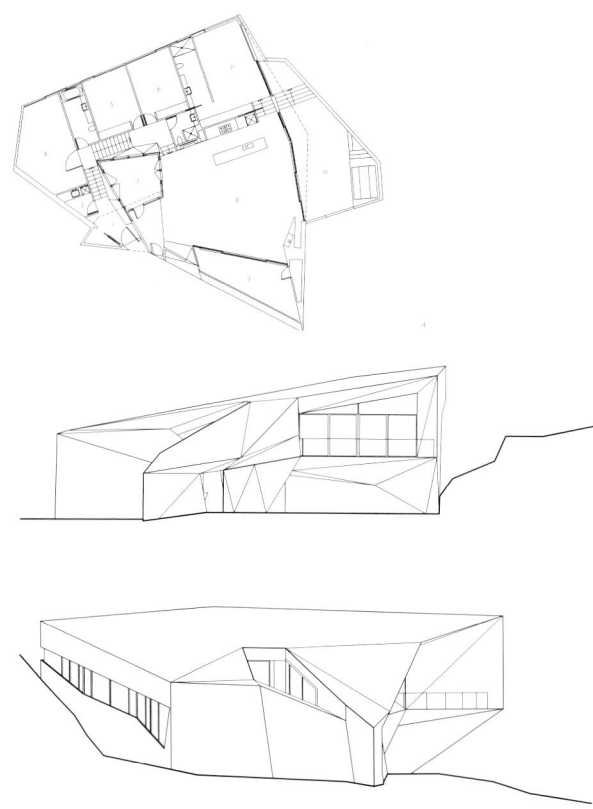

Leura House

A remarkable project, crowning a wonderful Blue Mountains vista, the Leura House unites fundamental 20th century ideas of open planning – of 'incomplete fluid space' – with a contemporary take on traditional Australian materials and construction techniques.

ARCHITECT : JAMES STOCKWELL

A remarkable project, crowning a wonderful Blue Mountains vista, the Leura House unites fundamental 20th century ideas of open planning – of 'incomplete fluid space' – with a contemporary take on traditional Australian materials and construction techniques. The design process began with James Stockwell's interest in 'discontinuous unity', a concept propounded by Japanese architects Junzo Sakakura and Takamasa Yoshizaka, and an idea that was to profoundly influence the domestic work of Le Corbusier, for whom they had worked. This idea conceived of space 'loosely'… without boundaries or defined thresholds, and as an interior journey punctuated by pauses and moments that might take the form of moveable or multifunctional walls, screens or structural elements. Space can be more open and it can flow between inside and out, or between one program and the next, in an organic and natural way.

The L-shaped plan of the Leura House is open to the northeastern valley aspect, and defining that 'L', a spine of 600mm rammed sandstone anchors the house into the land and becomes an ordering device for the series of internal spaces. Intended for a couple and their extended family – which includes 12 grandchildren – the planning provides for ample accommodation and bedrooms, and for a series of places that are either intimate and cosy, or expansive social areas that extend to the sweeping lawns and gardens. Each space is carefully designed to draw in light and to respond to solar and environmental concerns, and this aspect of the design is particularly inventive and resourceful. Both client and architect wanted a house that was essentially low-tech and that employed low-embodied energy materials, but that did so in such a way that the house could be constantly operable and functional: easily adjusted as the climate and mood required. Across the house, Stockwell has employed unprecedented constructional systems that enable this flexibility, including hatches in the verandas and walls that both ventilate and illuminate. The north-facing veranda itself is roofed by a huge pivoting plywood triangular prism that spans the veranda's entire length, and which adjusts to modulate the sunlight and rainfall. Curved plywood is then continued through the kitchen and the living spaces, creating a ceiling surface that folds the interior outwards to the light and air. Timber columns used in the loft employ a structural glass web to form a universal column, whilst the roof is built from carefully formed corrugated iron that, along with the timber, recalls local vernacular building tradition.

The material palette is relatively small and, to allow the materials and construction to be experienced and appreciated, elements are separated, or detailed in such a way that their structural purpose is revealed, and materials are often left raw and untreated. As the architect states, the design takes a "machine for living approach" to traditional Australian materials, creating a beautifully delicate and warm, yet highly functional dwelling.

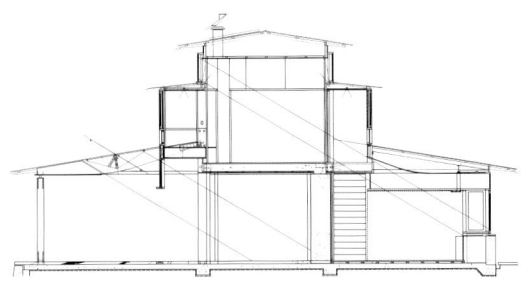
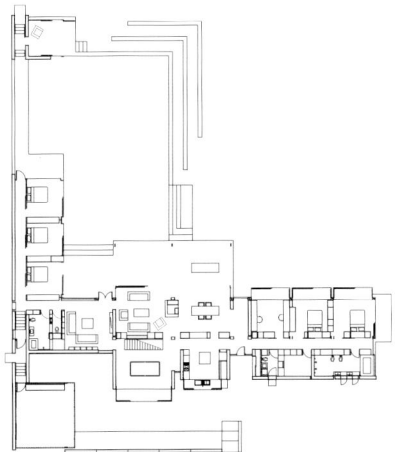

MACHANS BEACH COTTAGE

Formal desires are entirely motivated by the simplicity and charm of the original house, and then by the gentle rhythms of external circulation that weave between home and garden, and through the dense tropical ambience.

ARCHITECT : deb fisher

A post-war seaside cottage, a small community just north of Cairns in Far North Queensland, a love of gardens and an intense tropical climate were the basic ingredients for this remarkable piece of architecture. Formal desires were entirely motivated by the simplicity and charm of the original house, and then by the gentle rhythms of external circulation that weave between home and garden, and through the dense tropical ambience. The lessons in this dwelling are many and varied, not least those taken from the original cottage with its simple relationship to the street and the beachfront, and its subsequent significance for a small community. Deb Fisher's solution was to retain the existing building, treating the cottage as an extended veranda space and shifting the location of the kitchen and dining areas. New bedrooms, bathrooms and workrooms are then dispersed around a swimming pool and the luxuriant gardens, which were planned by Anton van der Schans. As Deb's partner, Suzanne Gibson observes, "The additions did not overwhelm the original cottage… the cottage sits lightly on the site, it's almost floating, it's beautiful." The 'compound' site plan is also an ideal response to the climate, maximizing the effectiveness of the southeast breezes, and the external circulation establishes an intimate relationship between the garden and house. The design and restoration of the garden was central to this project… the dwelling becomes an internalized private realm as well as a place to experience the ocean views.

Architecture in northern Queensland must respond to extreme environmental conditions: in addition to the seasonal downpours and summer heat, the location is subject to cyclones, corrosion and insect infestations (not to mention cane toads). The materials for this house were chosen to resist the effects of the sea air and wind, applied finishes were minimized, and construction techniques were kept to local applications, thus reducing cost and maintenance requirements. The new additions are raised above the '1 in 100 year' flood-line and the walkways are constructed from timber clad hot-dipped galvanized steel framing to control corrosion and termites.

Bright greens, reds and pinks are selectively applied throughout the design in contrast to the material severity, thus reinstating the palette of seaside cottages and complementing the tropical flora. The vividly coloured fibrous cement sheeting with expressed steel framing constitutes a cheerful reworking of humble seaside cottage construction. The Machans Beach Cottage is a delightful and unassuming residence that retains an established relationship with the beachfront, whilst enhancing the very lush qualities of the climate.

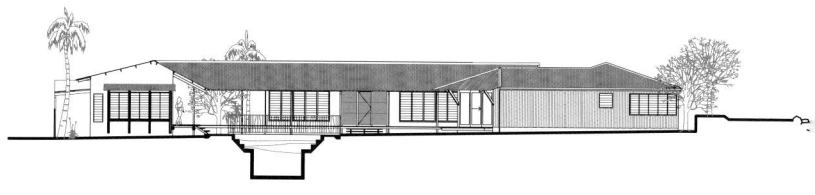
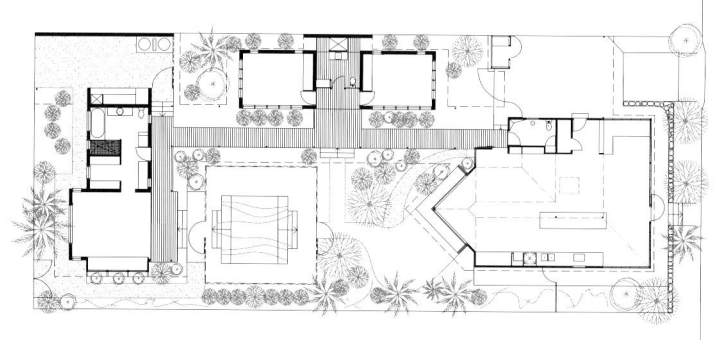

Australia's developing relationship with Asia is now as significant as its historical connection with Europe, so issues of 'place' and local architectural character have become increasing complex, and must now address not only indigenous and European histories, but also the reality of Australia's current cultural diversity.

ARCHITECT : ELIZABETH WATSON-BROWN

Ideas of place-making and architecture have a strong and rich history in Queensland: its climate, its beautiful landscapes and its early architectural history have created a context from which some of the most iconic images of Australian architecture have emerged. Elizabeth Watson-Brown is acutely aware of this history and its importance for contemporary place-making, however she has extended her vocabulary beyond the traditional Queensland vernacular to engage literally with the landscape... its physicality and its contours. Questions of an appropriate contemporary Australian identity are also addressed, especially in this house for a family (of Thai and Australian origin) who have returned to Australia after living for many years in Tokyo. Australia's developing relationship with Asia must now be seen to be as significant as its historical connection with Europe, so issues of 'place' and local architectural character have become increasing complex, and must now address not only indigenous and European histories, but also the reality of Australia's current cultural diversity. The climatic concerns of tropical Asian architecture are also relevant for much of the year in Queensland, as similar strategies are required to deal with storms, humidity, insects, extreme heat and the rapid weathering of materials. Sited in the rolling hills of Brookfield in the western suburbs of Brisbane, these issues find delightful expression in a family dwelling that incorporates an existing vernacular-style building.

The architectural *parti* is derived from a configuration of intimate pavilions that become part of the 'meta landscape' (literally an extension of the landscape) so that over time, the landscape and the architecture become one. The lines and geometry of the landscape extend to inform the planning and spatial configurations, and the site-plan becomes a mosaic... a regular dispersal of gardens, courtyards and simple enclosures. Raised up on timber platforms, the living spaces are oriented to maximize breezes and shade, whilst opening up and capturing particular site views. Flexibility and particularity – issues important for a family that required individual working and living zones, as well as shared space – are made possible through subtle shifts in the platform levels and with a variety of screening elements.

Watson-Brown's concerns of responding equally to both Asian and Australian cultural influences play out with the detailing and placement of the screens. The technique of framing internal off-white wall panels with thin timber strips recalls traditional Asian houses, and along with the incorporation of courtyards, the pyramidal roof forms, and the rhythms of finely created timber structural elements and screens, give the house a special identity and a most elegant physical beauty.

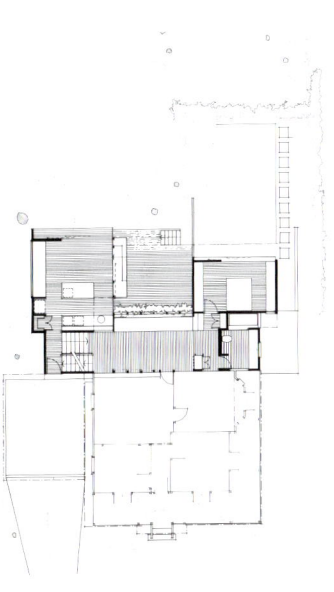

Questions of legibility and processes of manipulation are central to this design, and suggest how the architects went about cutting away and pixelating the original spherical form... how much can be removed with the form still remaining recognizable?

ARCHITECT : MCBRIDE CHARLES RYAN

In a manner that has become typical of McBride Charles Ryan, this three-bedroom house is a formally distinctive, playful and highly sculpted solution. Placed at the end of a cul-de-sac in Hawthorn, one of Melbourne's established suburbs, the house reads in sharp contrast to its neighbours. Without the more conventional driveway and garage, the building would not be recognisable as a house at all. From the street, the copper-clad domed form is only partially legible, and intentionally so. The architects, having a long-standing fascination with such platonic forms as the dome, began their design using a half sphere. Whilst the architects were not intentionally referencing Australian precedents, their dome does recall the work of Roy Grounds, and the less well known arched forms of Kevin Borland. As the architects say, "This is something we have worked with before… the idea of the single gesture, tampered with and then redistributed". The form of the building is thus a sphere, first sliced in Gordon Matta Clark fashion, with removed parts cast off and displaced across the site, thus becoming storage, a letterbox or seating.

Questions of legibility and processes of manipulation are central to this design, and suggest how the architects went about cutting away and pixelating the original spherical form… how much can be removed with the form still remaining recognizable? Continuing this process, the architects explored their interests in representation and contemporary digital technologies, but rather than use the computer to generate the building's form in a traditional manner, they were more interested in the idea of a pixel-made three-dimensional model. They speculated that if the original sphere were pixelated, it would have intriguing consequences for the curving façade and the interior. The final result reads like a puzzle and can be understood easily through this analogy.

In the process of building the idea, the architecture took on other influences. The pixelated moments in the project, which occur when openings, windows and doors break through the central sphere, recall the highly modelled and articulated surfaces of Carlo Scarpa. These redistributed 'pixels' also serve the architects in their intent to create a seamless transition between inside and outside: surfaces bleed from interior to exterior, and parts of the garden and exterior treatments are stitched back inside. This collage approach to textures, brick detailing and materiality is also a homage to Alvar Aalto's own Experimental House in Muuratsalo, Finland (1953).

This project extends the architects' interests beyond the purely formal into an engagement with the suburbs – particularly the growing disillusionment with the standard, white, modernist 'box' solution and the regressive sentimental re-enactment of bygone styles in pure facsimile. "What are the things that people are clinging onto?" they asked… "Turrets and texture!" The richly textured surfaces and articulated form of this house represent the architects' attempt to engage with the surrounding built context, and to develop a viable solution to enliven the dreariness of suburban housing.

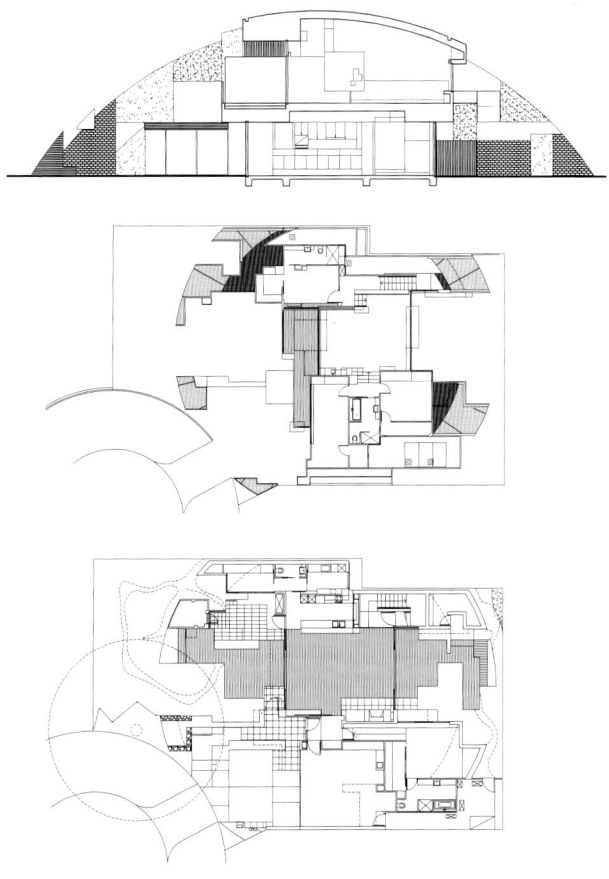

NORTHBRIDGE HOUSE

> This is an idea of architecture that is individualized not by the qualities of place, but rather by the relationship between the particular assemblage of elemental parts, the pragmatics and opportunities of industrialized prefabrication, and the rituals of inhabitation.

ARCHITECT : ALEX POPOV

The Northbridge House is a dwelling of contradictions and extremes, of light and dark, and of solids and voids. A modest single storey elevation presents to the street, and the house's polite appearance, sunk slightly below ground level, almost disappears into the neighbouring suburban context. An unassuming garage is pushed out slightly beyond the entrance and body of the house, and if it were not for the glimpse of intriguing vaulted forms disappearing down the northern side elevation, this first view of the house would be entirely unremarkable. Once beyond the portico and into the entry hall however, the house expands exponentially. Paired concrete rectangular columns, laid out like a car-park grid, form one structural system, which defines the space and supports the other principal system: a series of gently curved vaults running lengthways across the site. Inserted into this logic is an 18-metre lap pool, placed against the length of the vaults and pushed against the edge of the house, cantilevering out towards the view of Middle Harbour. Alex Popov's domestic architecture characteristically reflects his working knowledge of traditional Japanese houses, and here a centrally placed courtyard serves to draw light into the interior.

This pairing of columns and vaults as the structural *parti* of the house reflects the theories of 'additive systems,' which Popov discovered whilst working with Jørn Utzon. Popov recalls, "Utzon believed that in a modern industrialized society, one should be able to deal with housing in a sophisticated manner ... it doesn't have to be hand-sewn or labour intensive. One could develop a system of elemental components that can be added to progressively. Utzon urged to get away from the Miesian grid; you need more than one component, more than one steel grid, something that has the ability of being added to, so that the house has the possibility of growing in a linear pattern".

This is an idea of architecture that is individualized not by the qualities of place, but rather by the relationship between the particular assemblage of elemental parts, the pragmatics and opportunities of industrialized prefabrication, and the rituals of inhabitation. Unlike the modest façade, the interior is expansive and intentionally over-scaled, and the western one-storey entry volume becomes three storeys on the eastern side. This is an interior that needs to be lived in and traversed frequently, in order that one may become familiar with its many spatial sequences of voids, promenades and grand living areas. Though unmistakably a domestic project, its voluminous proportions and elemental materiality recall galleries and museums. For Popov, this issue is irrelevant, he does point out that Louis Kahn's vaulted Kimbell Art Museum, Fort Worth, USA (1972), was inspirational. Ironically, the Kimbell building was almost domestic in scale and ambience, challenging ideas of the museum experience. In the Northbridge House, traditional ideas of a domestic space, which are intimate and use a palette of 'warm' materials, are provoked. Important to this project is the concept of a spatial narrative in which one can disengage from busy city life, and into which one can fully retreat.

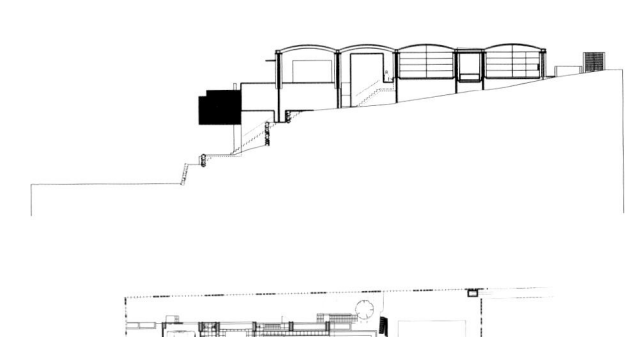
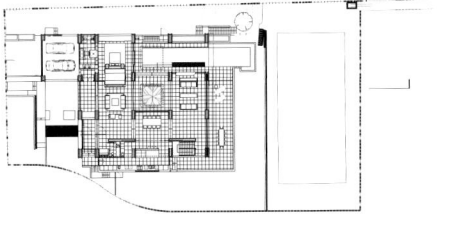
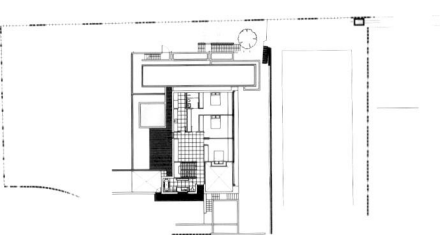

PERHAM RESIDENCE

This startling alteration and addition to a Victorian terrace in Sydney's inner-city suburb of Darlinghurst is a clear demonstration of what can be achieved in the heritage-listed streetscapes of Australia's cities.

ARCHITECT : SIMON HANSON - BUREAU SRH

This startling alteration and addition to a Victorian terrace in Sydney's inner-city suburb of Darlinghurst is a clear demonstration of what can be achieved in the heritage-listed streetscapes of Australia's cities. Whilst the existing building and the street-facing elevation are maintained, the rear western façade has been completely transformed as a contemporary expression of perforated plywood screens and flexible planning. This eye-catching rear elevation stands out from a typical motley collection of undistinguished terrace-house backsides, and emphatically demonstrates that heritage precincts can be enlivened, and that dreary back-lanes may indeed require such animation.

The separation between the existing house and the addition is clearly articulated by the insertion of a slim two-storey glass void, a glass staircase and a glass bridge. The physical and visual connection between the 'old' and the 'new' is more continuous in the planning and configuration of the ground floor, as the living room opens up from the (old) entry to a view of the (new) kitchen and rear courtyard beyond. Due to a steeply sloping site, the front entry and living room are elevated well above the street, creating a feeling of detachment, whilst at the room's other end, the experience is more intimate, slightly tucked away and sunken into the home's belly. The kitchen, raised above the living room, is very economical and efficient, with a seductive cocktail bar-like aesthetic of mirrors, stainless steel and linear lighting strips running between the exposed timber ceiling joists. The kitchen and dining room extend through a small backyard and carport to the rear laneway.

In contrast to this internalized ground floor experience, the upper levels comprise the bedrooms and a protected outdoor deck overlooking the city. It is at this point of connection and elevation that the architect's interest in digital technologies, the potential of CAD and laser cutting equipment, and rich but economical materiality is revealed. The patterned exterior screen plywood elements (achieved through Cad Cam) of the western façade, with a 1960s retro feel, are folded inside the house to become a staircase balustrade. Inserted next to the first floor stairs, a full-height storage system has been installed and coated with a high-gloss vivid red Two-Pac polyurethane paint finish, and with the light filtering in through the void and staircase, a brilliant red hue is omnipresent throughout the house. The new bedrooms are also internally clad with plywood, forming rather industrial interiors animated by aluminium and steel framing systems, and by the play of light and shadow through the balustrade's perforations. This delightful vertical display of colour and pattern also provides the domestic requirements of retreat, shelter and seclusion… albeit very inner-city and very *chic*.

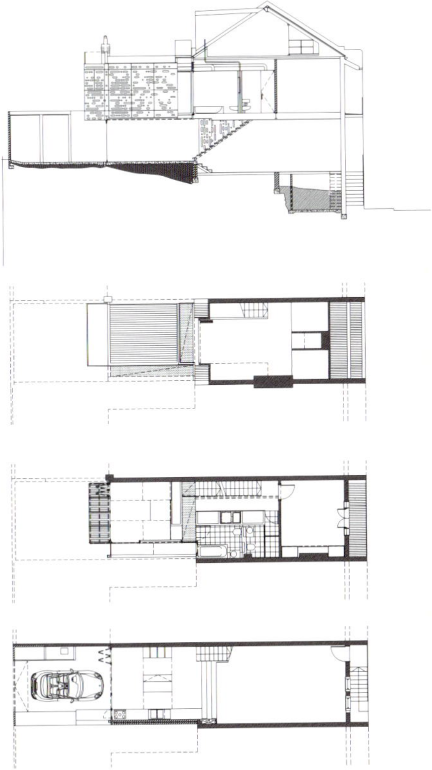

POINT PIPER HOUSE

For Louise Nettleton, the task of transforming what was a neglected and decaying building into a contemporary dwelling for a young family of four, was daunting.

ARCHITECT : LOUISE NETTLETON

This incredible house, overlooking Rose Bay from a terraced site in Point Piper, comprises a restoration and addition to a Hugh Buhrich house built in 1961. Buhrich – a German-born modernist architect, who completed a series of houses in Sydney between the late 1950s and the early 1970s, of which his Castlecrag House (1968-72) is the most well known – was a key figure in introducing a rather eclectic modernist style to Australia. Drawing on his time working with Hans Poelzig, Buhrich developed a style that synthesized his German expressionist tendencies with his love of Mies van der Rohe and the International Style. The Point Piper House stands apart from this synthesis: most notable for its extraordinary cantilevered living room and its extremely tall thin columns… this house expresses a kind of futuristic brutalism. For Louise Nettleton, the task of transforming what had become a neglected and decaying building into a contemporary dwelling for a young family of four, was daunting. Both client and architect agreed that the iconic elements – the cantilever and structural columns – must be maintained, however the interiors and the planning needed to be rethought, with the aim of admitting light into what was now a dark and cold house.

Nettleton's strategy was to rethink the circulation and planning, and then – most significantly – to insert a central garden courtyard that would bring northern light into the interior and provide ventilation. A circulation bridge and stairs were placed adjacent to this courtyard to open up views throughout the house, and the design utilizes the neighbouring mature landscapes to create the sensation, on the upper levels, of being in a tree house. This courtyard separates the public and private areas, as well as providing an equivalent to the backyard. The planning is direct and simple, and works from Buhrich's existing levels, apart from the addition of a bedroom, which is literally hung from the massive cantilevered slab. This insertion, secured to the columns with steel plates, is clad with glass and softly reflective zinc, and in keeping with Buhrich's tectonics, the language of this box is one of simple modernism elaborated with an almost industrial aesthetic. The intention was not to compete with the original, but rather to emphasize the dramatic gesture of the cantilever and the columns.

The entry sequence from the western street frontage has also been reworked: a paved entry courtyard was cut – as a threshold – into the original footprint, with an artist's studio to the south. The spatial sequence is linear, and Nettleton has emphasised this quality by delaying the view experience, and then by weaving a journey in and out of alternatively open and enclosed volumes that frame very particular moments of the surrounding context… leading to the jaw-dropping panoramic view.

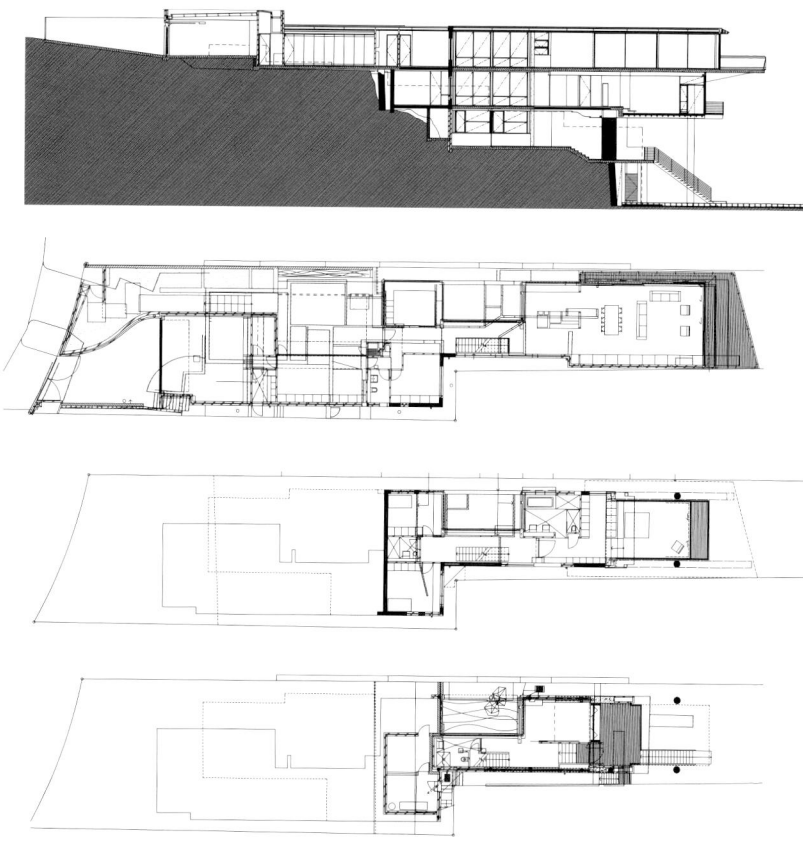

> The materiality, scale and layered composition intensify the experiential qualities of the gully landscape, and the construction – like the experience – appears ephemeral and wondrous.

ROSEBERY HOUSE

ARCHITECT : ANDRESEN O'GORMAN

The architectural *parti* of the Rosebery House is derived from a carefully orchestrated relationship between landscape and building in a secluded gully on the southern slopes of Highgate Hill, two kilometres south of the Brisbane CBD. Characterized by three layers of plant growth, the landscape of the gully creates its own interior of filtered light and deep shadows enclosed by large trees, saplings and vines. This micro-environment – along with the client's requirements for privacy – determined the evolution of a structure that mediated the relationship between landscape and building… resulting in a dwelling with various degrees of transparency and enclosure. The building form, whose orientation is intended to maintain the undulating gully space and to provide an equally scaled gesture, is a long narrow timber structure placed on the eastern slopes of the gully.

The two-storey porous structure is defined by a series of timber screens of alternate rhythms and density, which creates an interior space that continually adjusts and responds to shifts of light and temperature. An over-scaled battened screen placed between the lower contours of the gully landscape and the house itself serves as a mediating gesture, to establish points of 'coherence', and as a trellis for climbing plants. Seen across the gully, the domestic scale of the house – and its defining elements of doors, windows and balustrades – is thus concealed, partially blurred and transformed by the striated language of the timber screen. This screen, held slightly separate from the main dwelling, intensifies the experience of an expanded threshold. And, in keeping with this idea, planning is strung out along the length of the building: services and storage are tucked in at the back, whilst the public and living spaces open out to the landscape. Between the house and the screen is a mediating space, where transactions occur across the inhabited interior… a dappled internal landscape of modulated views, movements, lines, and degrees of sunlight and shadow. The materiality, scale and layered composition intensify the experiential qualities of the gully landscape, and the construction – like the experience – appears ephemeral and wondrous, with stained black timber elements providing the only possibility of structural legibility.

The influence of Andresen O'Gorman's architecture has been profound, and the Rosebery House is perhaps the most consummately implemented realization of their ideas and their research, which have been succinctly described by Philip Goad as "… a preoccupation with experimentation in domestic timber construction using indigenous Australian hardwoods… in combination with an approach to architecture that celebrates proportion, harmony and the deployment of human artifice in search of place: a proper sense of place in the Australian landscape".

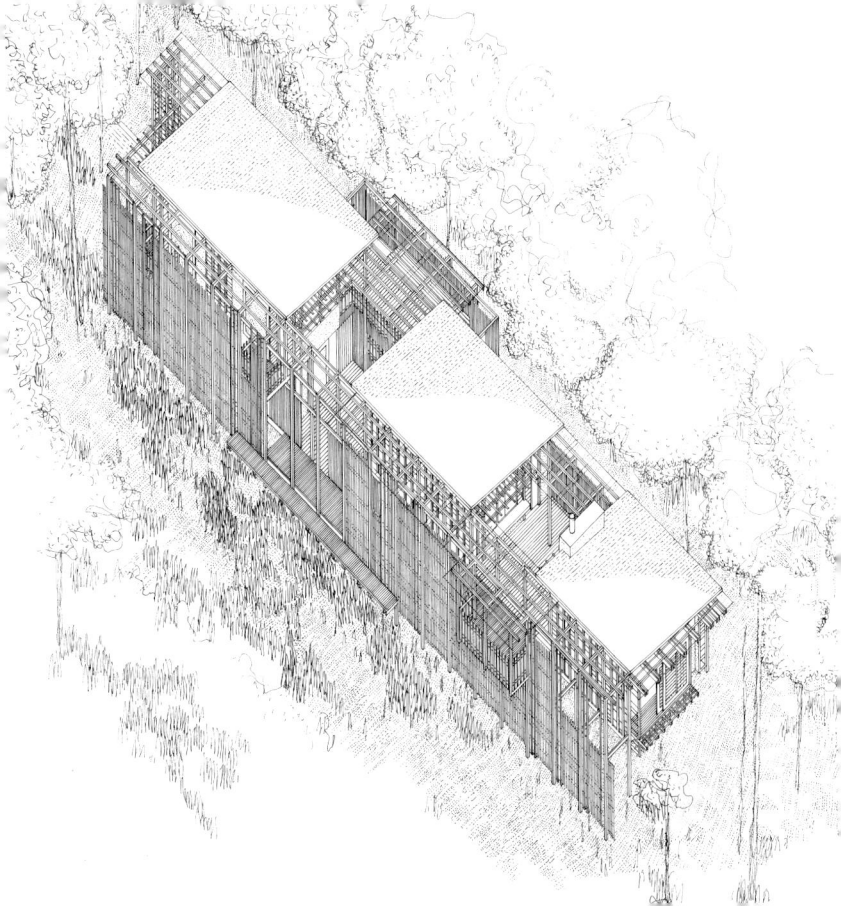

ROWNTREE STREET HOUSE

This addition, another one in Rex Addison's series of investigations into the vernacular, and a building without stylistic aspirations, is exemplary architecture. Equally a practical and a metaphorical composition, the project evidences a mastery of building and spatial gymnastics.

ARCHITECT : REX ADDISON

Continuing and extending Rex Addison's career-long exploration of local vernaculars, traditional building methods and roof forms, this inner-city project has manifested itself in sensual expressionist architecture. Increasing the floor area almost three-fold, the 2002 addition to an 1870s timber workers cottage with a pyramid roof comprises three levels vertically arranged at the rear of the site. The floor level of the original cottage is the spatial continuum within, pushing through to become the central zone of the addition, where a small kitchen and dining area steps up into the central living space. Below, on the garden level, is a studio with two bedrooms and a bathroom on the top floor. To accommodate these upper rooms, the addition rises up and slips back across the top of the old house in an axial way, echoing the slopes of the existing roof.

Addison's work is actively opposed to what he terms the modernist "carbuncle" approach to additions and alterations, where the 'new' pays no heed to the original and has the assertion of a unique higher order identity as its imperative. For Addison, "it is appropriate that the new building have a civilized discussion with the original… in musical terms, the design should play a tune in the same key rather than be discordant. It doesn't have to mimic the original, but improvize around the same tune". In this vein, whilst informed by the original geometries, Addison's addition can be experienced as an improvization, which takes familiar key motifs of the original and develops them into singular and varied elaborations, expressed with a series of delightful transgressions. The roofline of the addition, stepping out with plywood eaves and corrugated iron roofing at each level to provide shelter for external spaces below, is easily recognizable as continuing a vernacular concerned with traditional Australian building forms and construction.

The interior is lined seamlessly throughout in warm toned plywood, with expressed roof members and a timber floor that displays the tone and the grain of the end-matched mixed species. The plasticity of Addison's details, as they wrap and curve around plumbing and servicing, then drop to form bulkheads, and turn and fold to form nooks, shelving and seating is much less precedented… certainly in an Australian context. This interior architecture is more expressionist, almost lyrical in tune. The rich intensity of the material palette, and the adroitness and investment in the craft of building recall both Rudolf Schindler's Studio-Residence in West Hollywood (1922), and Addison's own House and Studio in Brisbane (1999).

There is a quiet audaciousness to this work, and Addison wholeheartedly resists the modernist approach, as well as the postmodernist "headlong rush for rhetoric". Throughout his architectural education in the 1960s, he was immersed in Frank Lloyd Wright, Schindler, and the Arts and Crafts movement. He is far less interested in building an idea than in "an idea about a building". This addition, another one in Addison's series of investigations into the vernacular, and a building without stylistic aspirations, is exemplary architecture. Equally a practical and metaphorical composition, the project evidences a mastery of building and spatial gymnastics. It is of another kind altogether to the more familiar descriptions of contemporary dwelling.

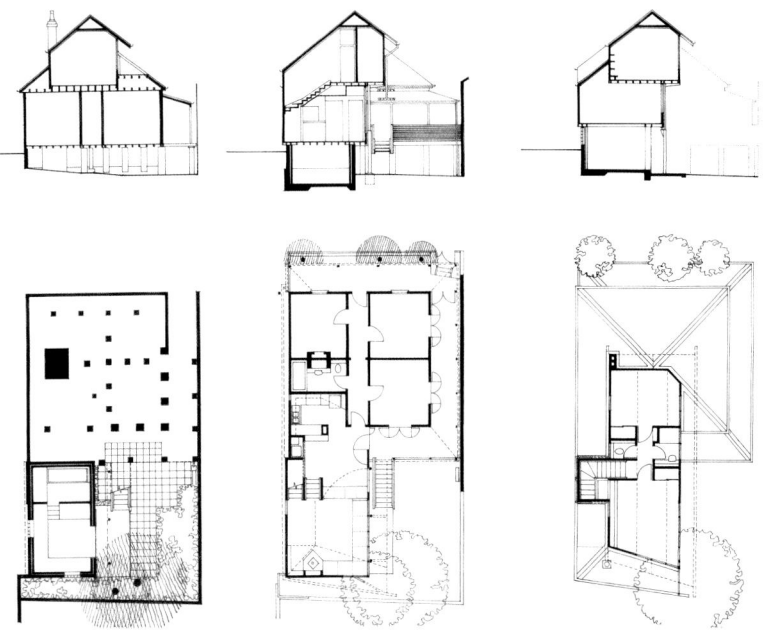

SPRINGWATER

Springwater, one of Peter Stutchbury's most significant projects, demonstrates spatial, volumetric and constructional mastery... more extraordinary however, is the architectural dexterity shown by the architect.

ARCHITECT : PETER STUTCHBURY

Conceived of as a 'reliable camp', Springwater's occupation of site is alternatively commanding and delicate, accommodating in its rhythms of solid and void, and of platforms and structure, that mark out a pattern for dwelling. Concrete – imperfect and raw – is left to reveal its material and constructional properties, and is formed into slender rectangular volumes that reach across a site – populated with the twisting limbs of angophora trees – sloping down to Sydney's Middle Harbour. Polished timber contrasts with this severity, running along balustrade handrails, window-frames and door-frames.

Springwater, one of Peter Stutchbury's most significant projects, demonstrates spatial, volumetric and constructional mastery… more extraordinary however, is the architectural dexterity shown by the architect. With his direct connection to the Pittwater Set (arguably the next generation of the Sydney School), and most notably Richard Leplastrier and Bruce Rickard, and with his experience of the functional building tradition as seen at his family's rural property, Peter Stutchbury is intimately engaged with a dialogue between architecture and place, and between climate and a vernacular tradition. This is an idiom that has often been characterized by an identifiable and sometimes clichéd expression, but Stutchbury's work transcends this characterization and offers something more abstracted and sculptural, and less reliant on a direct quotation of vernacular models. A clue to Stutchbury's suppleness of approach lies in his interest in Jørn Utzon and the elemental idea of Platforms and Plateaus. In many of Stutchbury's earlier houses (such as the Clareville House, 1999) this was translated into forms driven by literal or metaphorical reference – for example, a bird's wing becomes a roof – but with Springwater all obvious references are removed… leaving what Stutchbury describes as "basic bottom-line aesthetics".

Springwater draws on the modernist lessons of purist abstraction and of fluid exchange between inside and outside, yet this is not the only explanation for Stutchbury's 'moves' here, which are not style driven… rather, they are a response to his intimate search for connection between land and people, and between architecture and place. Unlike many of his previous houses, this project is devoid of overt technological accoutrements, and is a more elemental response to living. Planning is simple and refined: two primary volumes – set above each other on the steeply falling site – frame a series of platforms, courtyard spaces and an outdoor kitchen. The lower volume – a gallery, which also doubles as the main bedroom – acts as a counterpoint to the upper volume, which contains the public living spaces on its ground level below a series of bedrooms on the first floor. The living areas can be completely opened, in keeping with the idea that the house can become an open frame through which sunlight, breezes, and the scents of the bush-land can pass. Springwater thus operates as a series of tensions and contrasts between heaviness and lightness, mass and void… and ultimately between nature and architecture.

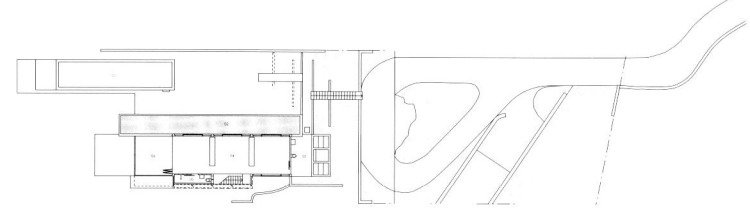
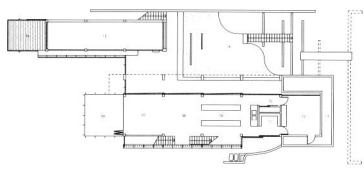
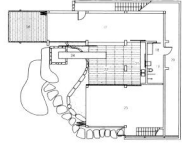

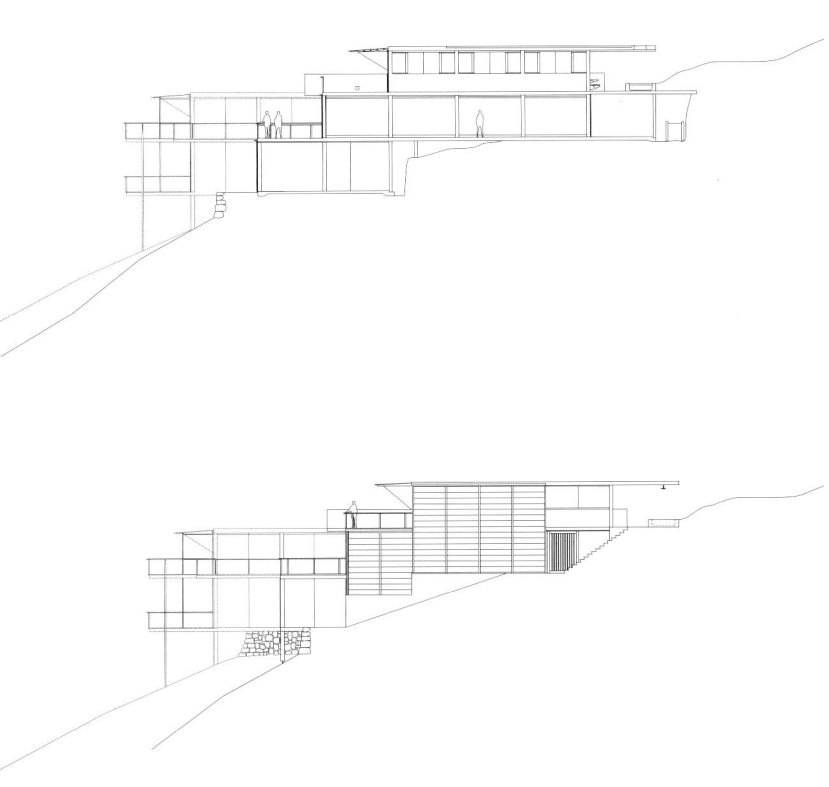

SPRY HOUSE

Whilst this house responds wonderfully to its particular climate and views, the architectonics are not of Australian origin nor do they aspire to a particular image of Australian domesticity. Rather, the formal language recalls modernist strategies of the floating timber box, as explored by Alvar Aalto among others.

ARCHITECT : durbach block

The Spry House at Point Piper is, as Neil Durbach says, a "more geometrically overwrought building" than Durbach Block's Holman House (completed in the same year). This three storey house, curving both in plan and in section, is directed down the site towards the views of Sydney Harbour. The plan is composed of three elements: a pool, a courtyard, and the gently twisting, or – as the architects describe it – "slumped" form of the house. All three elements run in parallel, creating a passage through both site and house.

Whilst this house responds wonderfully to its particular climate and views, the architectonics are not of Australian origin nor do they aspire to a particular image of Australian domesticity. Rather, the formal language recalls modernist strategies of the floating timber box, as explored by Alvar Aalto among others. Durbach confesses to thinking that "the Pittwater set [and] the Sydney School have an almost didactic position of what is Australian architecture," which he finds "stifling, and not a fascinating game to play".

From the courtyard, the body of the house reads as a homogenous edge, with strips of 20 mm glass worked between timber battens, enabling blue-toned light to penetrate the interior. This edge creates a single curving gesture, which then floats on a glass base. The twist in plan admits the exterior landscape and light to the kitchen and dining room areas. The body of the house rises from below ground level through the upper two storeys, expanding access to the views. Highly figured skylights, or "fissures" as Durbach calls them, cut through from the roof, bringing light into the first floor bathroom and bedroom spaces. These sculptural voids, folded and angled in plan, become skylights in the ground floor ceiling.

In contrast to these aspiring geometric plays, a modest façade presents to the rear southern street-facing elevation and, as with the Holman House, conceals the spatial drama that lies within. Pushed hard up against the site boundary, the eastern side of the building bends in section and away from its neighbours, responding to council setback regulations. Whilst the rest of the building curves in plan-form only, this wall expands the geometric dialogue, curving twice along its height. Rising from below ground, the wall leans in towards the main body of the house but never quite touches it, allowing the placement of a skylight that illuminates the circulation points between levels. The rear entrance is also placed into this architectural gap.

Despite the almost excessive geometric explorations of previously unexplored ideas, this house – with its "tottering form" drifting across the site – is, in the words of Durbach, "a delicate proposition".

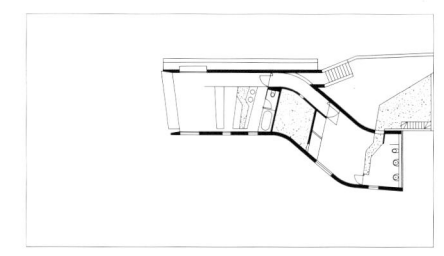

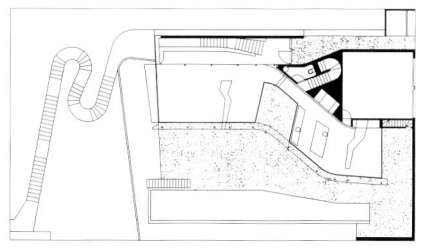

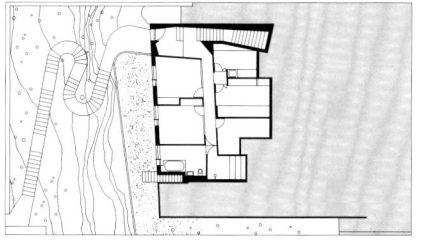

STANWELL PARK HOUSE

This house speaks of a long-standing tradition of Australian domestic architecture, engaging with imagery and constructional techniques specific to the temperate east coast, whilst possessing an almost spiritual quality of dwelling, enhanced by allusions to the Japanese temple form.

ARCHITECT : CASEY BROWN

Located at the base of the spectacular Stanwell Park escarpment south of Sydney, with views overlooking the beach and the Pacific Ocean, this house continues a set of clearly defined and expressed ideas seen in previous Casey Brown projects, such as the James Robertson House (2001) at Mackerel Beach. Clearly evident is the practice's appreciation and understanding of the craft of building and the phenomenal possibility of materiality. In this house, designed for several families to holiday together, a continuing attention to detail and an exploration of materiality – alternatively lightweight and transparent, then solid and sculptural – are revealed. Materials are selected to withstand the seaside conditions, but also to recede into the landscape, to become one with the surrounding native vegetation. As seen in the James Robertson House, the roof form adopts an aesthetic of fallen leaves… of corrugated copper roof planes coming together and extending over enclosures to provide shelter from the rain and sun.

Casey Brown continue their exploration of dwelling as a relationship of events, spaces and forms within which the domestic narrative plays out. However, unlike the dispersed forms of the James Robertson House, the pavilions at Stanwell Park are brought together… linked in a layered plan-form that shifts and adjusts in response to the views and climatic conditions, whilst addressing various requirements for privacy and for social gatherings. Two twisting internal staircases – described as "Escher stairs" by architect Rob Brown – descend from the main living area to link the living pavilions, and level changes demarcate the functional differences, which are orientated to catch the cooling northeast sea breezes. Decks extend from all living spaces to enable an outdoor living experience all year round.

Central to Casey Brown's architecture is the journey towards the residence. At Stanwell Park, a long boardwalk path leads from an exposed street position to the main entry, sheltered by the house's southern stone wall. Massive walls, establishing a counterpoint to what is otherwise a lightweight finely detailed structure, continue through the house and form solid boundaries to the central living spaces. Speaking of a long-standing tradition of Australian domestic architecture, this palatial house engages with imagery and constructional techniques specific to the temperate east coast, whilst possessing an almost spiritual quality of dwelling, enhanced by allusions to the Japanese temple form.

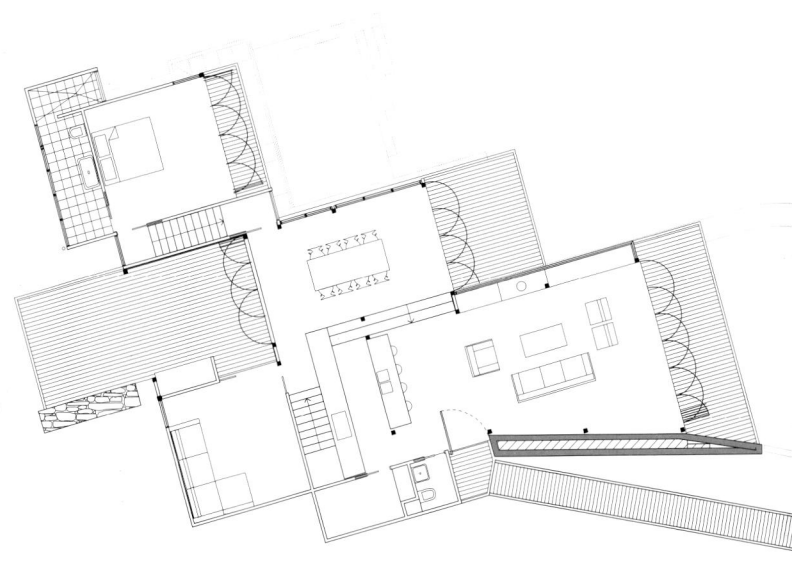

SWAN STREET RESIDENCE

The result of this investigation, apart from some provocative architecture, is a series of devices that offer opportunities to 'recalibrate'... to rework the way in which suburban houses function and how they respond to context.

ARCHITECT : iredale pedersen hook

The Swan Street Residence – the 'Swan Song' – can be seen as the culmination of backyard renovation projects completed by Iredale Pedersen Hook over the past 10 years. This process has explored, perhaps even exploited, the potential of the renovation in Perth's suburbs. The result of this investigation, apart from some provocative architecture, is a series of devices that offer opportunities to 'recalibrate'… to rework the way in which suburban houses function and how they respond to context. Categories of investigation include ideas of the opportunistic suburb, a referential landscape, the means of economy, the environmental construct and social sustainability. When brought together, these ideas translate into projects that work directly with suburban regeneration and densification, and with the potential of the existing building. The 'economy' dictates a reconfiguration of the 'old' so that it responds to northern orientation, to the surrounding context and to the requirements of contemporary living. The 'poetic' then emerges from how architectural form might be achieved within these limitations… form and spatial experiences emerge from the rescaling and abstracting of contextual elements.

These ideas converge at Swan Street in a dwelling that speaks externally of its contextual material relationships, and internally of a spatial narrative that recalls memories – relevant to the client and the architects – of landscape, qualities of light and dreamy spatial progressions. This duality of experience – what the architects call the 'Jekyll and Hyde' quality – was then carried through into the material selection: the picket fence, the metal roof, oiled recycled jarrah battens, and copper cappings, all of which, in the process of weathering, yield to the context. References to the remaining Arts and Crafts houses of the established eastern suburbs of Perth can be detected in the proportions and timber detailing of the façade. The green polycarbonate and the stained plywood cladding evoke other sensations and recollections… more abstract and ephemeral, when the interiors shift and alter as sunlight shines through the polycarbonate.

The folding roof is a continuation and exaggeration of the surrounding roof-scape, and its draped form allows for an extended interior journey that graduates the transition from 'old' to 'new', and to the backyard and pool. The spontaneous – almost emotional – expressionist appearance of the project, when seen from the street, can perhaps be explained by Adrian Iredale's candid confession… "Late in the design process, and after a glass of red wine, I 'revisited' Hans Scharoun's Philharmonie [Berlin, 1963], resulting in a frenzied redesign… and the project as it exists today". The success of this renovation (and of this practice) has been achieved by a combination of pragmatics, economy, rich poetic ideas and an extensive architectural knowledge.

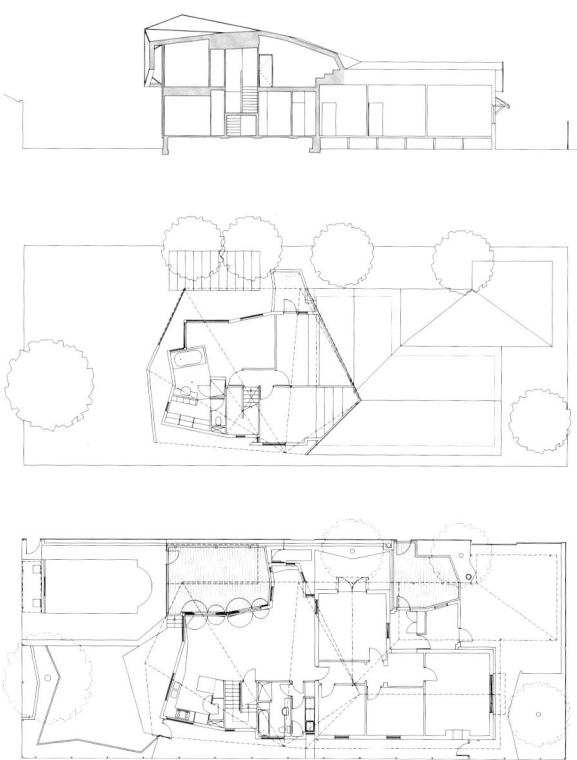

TIBET GALLERY

This is an architecture whose beauty and success comes not through grand size and volumes, expensive materials and finishes, but rather through the very best of what architecture can be... invention, delight and economy.

ARCHITECT : donovan hill

The Tibet Gallery is a modest project that belies a programmatic and formal complexity. Prior to alteration, the existing building – an original Victorian terrace house – contained the clients' gallery and workspace, and after the birth of their son, the couple decided to make their workplace their home as well. The architects' task was thus doubly complex, to accommodate both a gallery with workspace and storage, and a two-bedroom dwelling within a context that has stringent council heritage overlays. Having known one of the clients since their university days, Timothy Hill of Donovan Hill knew the spatial and architectural configuration that would be suitable. Responding to the clients' Nepalese background and the gallery's hand woven Tibetan rugs, the architects' work is central Asian in tone and inspires a ritualistic spatial narrative. Delicate timber screens frame structures and shelving, and veils of silken material weave their way through the old terrace house. Almost diagrammatic in its application, the timber wraps around floors and walls, then turns to become seating, shelving or storage. These gestures work over and through the existing site, framing moments of the original or simply hovering close to the aged textures and surfaces. Such is the delicacy of the architecture that the addition appears to caress the old building, and in doing so, creates a space almost sacred in ambience.

Very little could be altered in the two front rooms at street level, so the new work is held between the existing structures: a screen, clad in handmade paper, folds around the gallery space, whilst timberwork wraps around doorways and hovers just above the ground to form display areas. Moving into the rear of the project, the floor level steps up and into a decked outdoor area, and along this progression from inside to out, the timberwork becomes even lighter and more delicate. A long slim fishpond runs between the 'new' and the 'old', and above this, a glass wall supported by timber frames an old blockwork wall. A heavy timber door with an overscaled frame leads to the first floor, and demarcates public and private. Another dialogue is introduced in this upper storey… here the architects treat the original in a more playful manner, at times mimicking details and drawing attention to certain particularities: a masonry archway is extended, contrasting with the modern addition; and the silhouette of a stairway banister or cornice detail becomes an outline for a detail of the new. The private realm, consisting of two very small bedrooms, a bathroom, a living room, a kitchen and a study, continues the rhythm of timber battens, delicate detailing and the flirtation with the existing building.

The centre of the domestic space is the living room. Stepping up into the room, an overhead void opens ups the small floor area, whilst intimate views towards the backyard increase the room's protective, womblike quality. Again timber wraps up the walls, forming shelves and special pockets for *objets d'art*. Using and touching the screens, the handles and the shelves, brings another dimension to the project: one that is sensorial and ritualistic, where the cumulative effect is to invoke essential memories of shelter and enclosure, and what it is to live comfortably in space. This is an architecture whose beauty and success comes not through grand size, expensive materials and finishes, but rather through the very best of what architecture can be… invention, delight and economy.

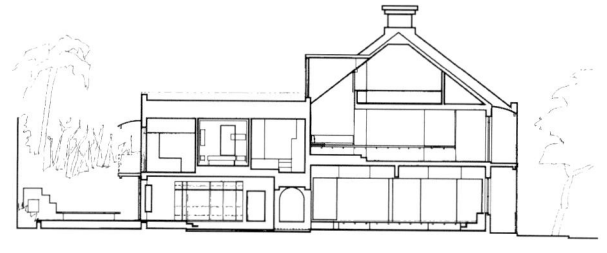
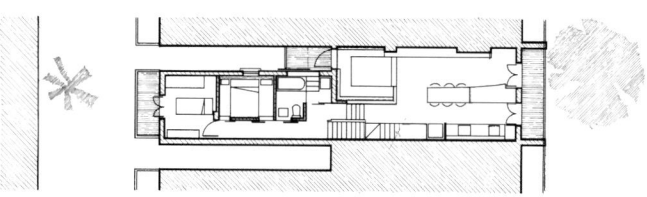
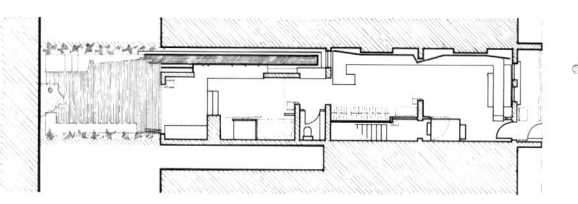

TYSON STREET HOUSE

In the dense urban fabric of Richmond, just to the east of Melbourne's **CBD**, Jackson Clements Burrows were faced with a plethora of constraints and limitations, however this prompted an ingenious solution that challenges notions of heritage propriety and appropriateness.

ARCHITECT : jackson clements burrows

For architects designing houses in the overwhelmingly urban context of inner-city precincts, issues of heritage preservation, and of what is permitted or prohibited in terms of architectural expression, are paramount. The importance of conserving buildings of architectural or historical significance cannot be underestimated, but what should be preserved and the degree of restriction on developments is a matter of quite some debate. In the dense urban fabric of Richmond, just to the east of Melbourne's CBD, Jackson Clements Burrows were faced with a plethora of constraints and limitations, however this prompted an ingenious solution that challenges accepted notions of heritage propriety and appropriateness. The streetscape comprised an eclectic mix of workers cottages protected by a municipal heritage overlay, which included their client's decaying single-fronted weatherboard dwelling. Council advisors argued that this existing house contributed to the heritage streetscape and, therefore, any addition or alteration must take heed of that context in terms of scale, form and detail.

In a provocative gesture – one that critiqued the very process – the architects imposed a 1:1 photographic image, printed on glass, of the original house and context on to the street façade of what is now a completely modern dwelling. This solution addressed the requirements of heritage regulations, but also satisfied the client's desire for as expedient a process as possible. The final vision becomes a kind of *simulacra* loaded with irony and provocation, a strange blurring of new and old, which creates an uncanny sensorial experience… and behind this façade, the architecture that unfolds is entirely contemporary in its expression.

Looking back from the rear garden, the house is seen as a crisp and modern two-storey dwelling that works efficiently with the narrow site conditions and provides for a series of open light-filled interior spaces. As the owner states, "People ask how I cope with living behind a giant photograph, but I've forgotten all about the photo". Of particular interest is the spatial complexity of the transition from the street entry to the first floor and its outdoor deck. Here the architectural language shifts – literally – to become an off-white translucent polycarbonate that folds around the staircase to enclose the upper bedroom level. With its geometric fluidity and clever application of material, this gesture speaks of another reading of Richmond's history – that of small industrial buildings and factories – and in doing so, mediates the highly contemporary front elevation with the rear's more traditionally modernist expression.

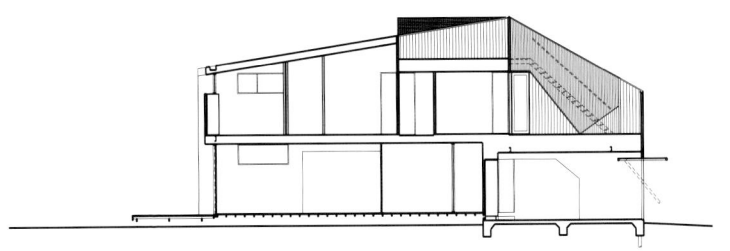
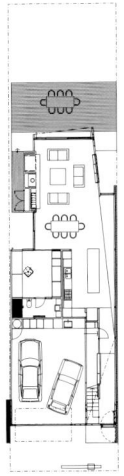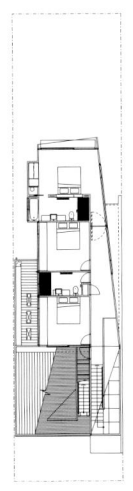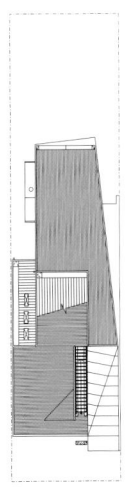

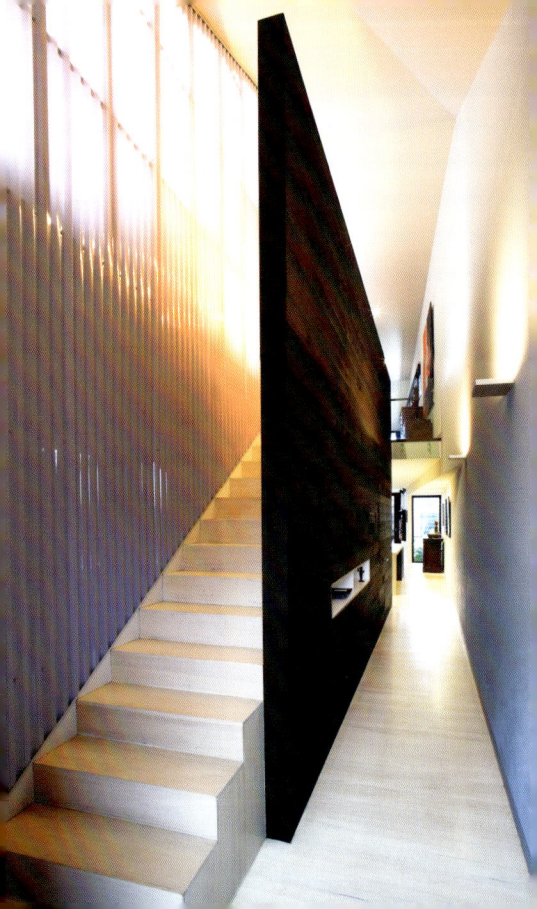

VINEYARD HOUSE

Composed of rammed earth, timber and steel, this house possesses an expressionist plasticity that, set against the precise tempo of the adjacent vineyard, establishes the architectural *parti*.

ARCHITECT : joHN WARdLE

Situated within a large stand of Manna Gums and Stringy Barks overlooking the lush farming country of Victoria's Mornington Peninsula, this house, composed of rammed earth, timber and steel, possesses an expressionist plasticity that, set against the precise tempo of the adjacent vineyard, establishes the architectural *parti*. The winegrower's practice of grafting new cultivars onto existing rootstock established the organic diagram that drives the plan form of the house, giving formal expression to the clients' shift from the city to the country, and the consequent integration of their public viticultural activities with their domestic life.

The architectural expression takes its lead from the over-scaled rammed-earth walls at the entry, and the similarly robust timber framing that shields the northern living spaces. A centrally placed orthogonal wall forms the spine of the building, initiating the domestic narrative and leading directly into the 'socializing' north-facing living spaces. The kitchen and scullery form the divide between public and private. Once past that threshold, the private realm stretches south along the other side of the main wall, before curving outwards and away from the body of the house, following the original 'viticultural' diagram. This progression climaxes within the master bedroom, which is aligned to provide intimate views of the surrounding landscape.

Whilst the rammed-earth in this project represents a new material application for John Wardle, the architectonics of the project are familiar, continuing explorations begun in earlier works. Elements of materiality and an expressed structural system pull out and elaborate upon contextual features, whilst the form pivots and twists to align with desired views. The eastern elevation is dominated by two 'secateured ends'... a custom-made massive steel framing system holds the slanting floor-to-ceiling glass walls in place, and one of the cut 'ends' shows the master bedroom, whilst the other displays the living room. 'Misaligned'... these 'end' forms are orientated away from each other and towards their own particular vistas. Manipulated steel elements are also used for the entry canopy, which, clipped over the top of the earth wall, unfolds like origami down the wall's elevation to form the sheltering entrance gesture.

The internal detailing of the timber ceilings and wall panels is similarly highly designed, revealing expressively scaled-down moments of the overall form. Door handles are personalized, as are light fittings, built-in seating and a highly sculpted cabinet for the fireplace. In contrast, the rammed-earth walls remain 'untouched' and relatively pure elements, as all reveals are kept free of window details or servicing. The house becomes an organism in and of itself, each part continuing and re-expressing an original DNA. Though not quite a 'machine for living', the Vineyard House is a highly orchestrated project with a defining presence, both as an object in the landscape and as a richly layered internal volume.

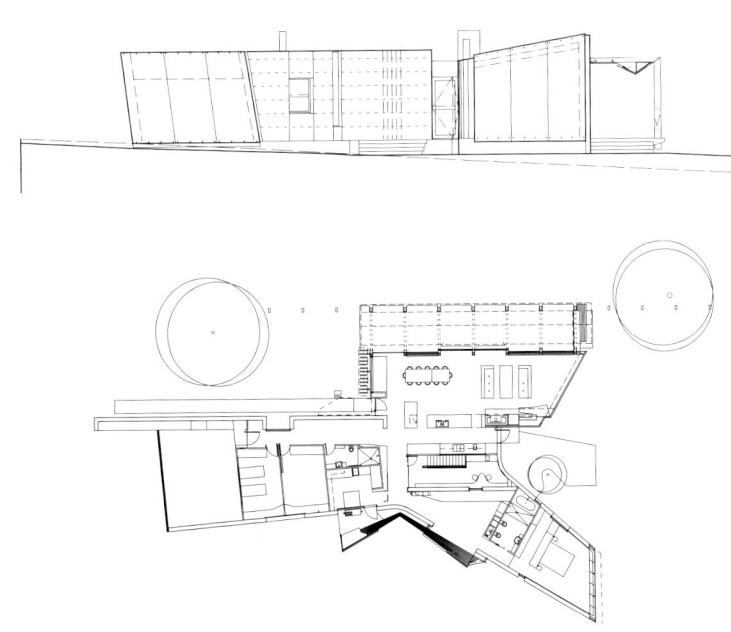

wallaby way house

For Troppo, "true sustainability remembers what it is like to value 'place'"… and 'place-making' encompasses issues of climate and identity, but it also addresses how people engage with their space, their surroundings and the landscape.

ARCHITECT : TROPPO QUEENSLAND

Designing for environmental and social sustainability has been fundamental to the work of Troppo Architects since their inception in Darwin in 1981. With their pioneering approach to connecting directly with the specific requirements of building in a harsh and distinctly Australian landscape, the practice has engaged – intimately, thoroughly and productively – with core issues of sustainability, and their ultimate aim is to be climatically and culturally responsive. Underpinning this ideology is a serious questioning and investigation of what sustainability might consist of, beyond a set of codes, date, regulations and rules. For Troppo, "true sustainability remembers what it is like to value 'place'"… and 'place-making' encompasses issues of climate and identity, but crucially, it also addresses how people engage with their space, their surroundings and the landscape. The Wallaby Way House is a precise example of how these ideas play out at the scale of domestic architecture, resulting in a meaningful, and almost parsimonious, enclosure.

Although located on tropical Magnetic Island, off the coast of Townsville in northern Queensland, the site is dominated by a dense pine-forest, and the building is arranged to accommodate those existing trees. The form of the house is simple and elemental: it is essentially a rectangular block whose threshold conditions between inside and outside are entirely permeable and flexible. Living and bedroom spaces are centrally located and extend out onto the veranda and the outdoor living spaces. Continuing the refined elemental approach, circulation is direct, and follows a cruciform path across and through the internal verandas, strategically revealing views and particular moments within the landscape. Materials are lightweight with a low mass and, in conjunction with the operable walls, the building requires no air-conditioning: it is entirely responsive to, and embracing of, the climate. Steel and timber are the predominant materials, with a steel portal frame and roofing, which allow for the generous internal spans and wide overhangs, and provide protection during the cyclone season. Renewable timber – detailed in a single-skin system – is used for the cladding of walls, floors and ceilings, and allows for minimal material consumption and maximum dynamic thermal performance.

In true Queensland fashion, the house is raised 1.5 metres above ground level, giving a sense of privacy and protection for the owners. The roof form dominates the architectural expression – characteristic of Troppo (and fellow influential exponents of lightweight architecture, such as Gabriel Poole and Russell Hall) – and works to create dynamic interior spaces… either sheltered and intimate, or open and voluminous. To live in this house is to experience the landscape, the climate and the environment (and domesticity) in a simple and essential way.

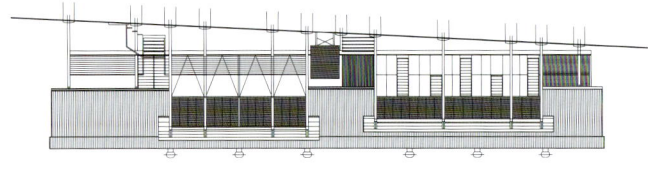

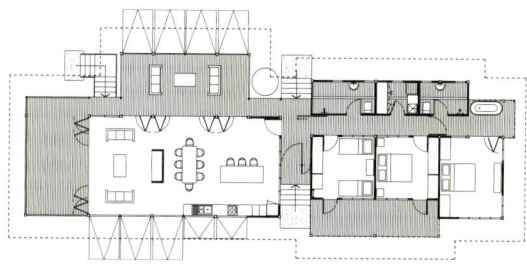

WHALE BEACH

This luxuriously crafted beach house, north of Sydney on the Barrenjoey Peninsula, is further demonstration of an evolution that has occurred in Alex Popov's recent domestic work, and of a corresponding shift in Sydney's architectural identity... from lightweight pavilions to a more robust and grounded expression.

ARCHITECT : ALEX POPOV

This luxuriously crafted beach house, north of Sydney on the Barrenjoey Peninsula, is further demonstration of an evolution that has occurred in Alex Popov's recent domestic work, and of a corresponding shift in Sydney's architectural identity… from lightweight pavilions to a more robust and grounded expression. This house possesses the same highly resolved assembly found in his Northbridge House (completed three years earlier, in 2003), but the 'kit of parts' has altered. This house expresses a clear orthogonality, with precedents in Spanish and Italian modernism. The vault forms of the Northbridge House and the Rockpool Apartments (1999), at Mona Vale, have gone… as have the expressionist steel structures, replaced here by a more refined, abstracted monumentality and a newfound simplicity.

An economical *parti* of massive parallel concrete walls holds a rectangular volume defined by thick concrete slabs and equally thick black timber-clad walls. A narrow site with a dramatic slope, falling away in a sheer drop to the ocean, presented the immediate problem of admitting light into the interior… one which was solved by detaching the perimeter walls from the central volume, thus drawing in sunlight. Whilst a glass breezeway corridor is placed into the gap between the wall and the house on the southern side, the break is left as a void space on the north, framing the main entrance and allowing light into the living spaces. The window openings are frameless apertures, articulated by cuts made directly into the primary skin. Popov's love of materiality softens these strict geometries and planar surfaces, as recycled timber cladding – in the form of narrow strips finished in black – continues from the exterior into the interior. The exposed concrete ceilings and the in-situ walls are rubbed by hand with soda water – a technique used on the shells of the Sydney Opera House – to achieve a velvety soft 'buttery' feel, and American oak flooring is used to provide warmth and contrast.

The interior has an intimacy of scale, and the spaces feel unquestionably domestic. The spatial rhythm is one of moving down and into the house, and a sense of compression is maintained throughout, expanding only at the periphery, where the house opens out: horizontally to the deep blue of the Pacific Ocean; and vertically to the double-height void space above the living room. In keeping with all Popov's architecture, the roof form is fundamental… here it is completely flat and recedes from the dominant slab and wall lines. As Popov says, "I didn't want to elicit the same flyaway roof that had been done here [in Whale Beach] before, so we worked towards expressing another way of dealing with roof-scape from the street… it is simply a flat plane, as if you had put your hand on it and squashed it down". The Whale Beach House presents a forceful, monumental and abstract contrast to the surrounding 'flyaway' pavilions to which Popov refers, and – with its thick black timber cladding – reinstates a Sydney northern beaches residential typology that dates back to the early 20th century houses of James Peddle and Alexander Stewart Jolly.

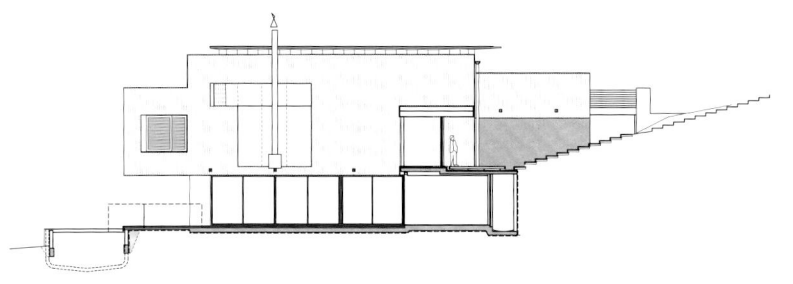
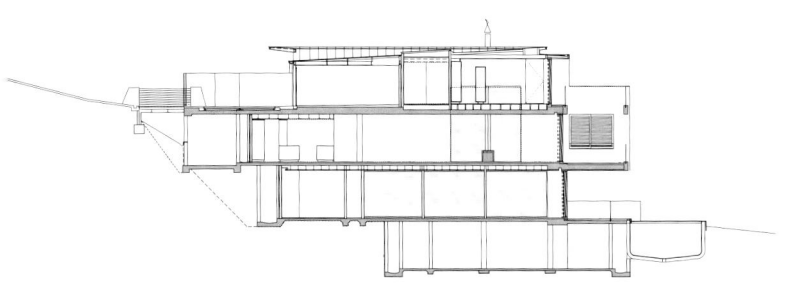

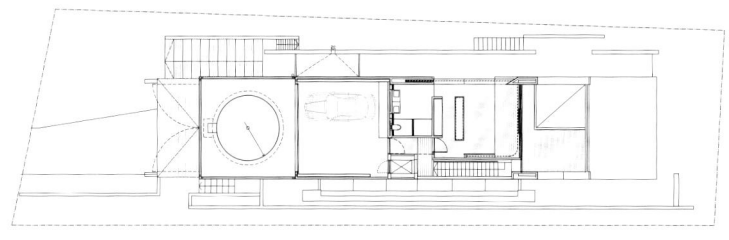

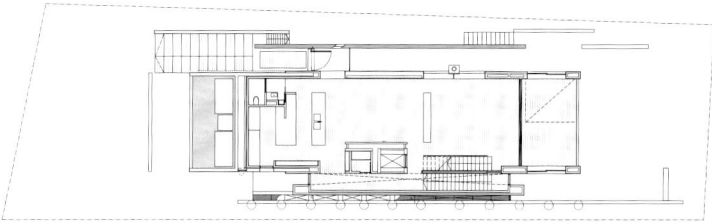

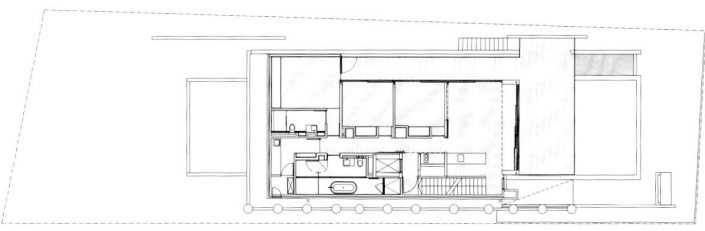

WHEATSHEAF HOUSE

As with Phillip Johnson's Glass House and Ludwig Mies van der Rohe's Farnsworth House, this building is raised off the ground on a broad plinth. Jesse Judd's pavilion, held taut with black steel columns, is a quirky revision of that orthogonal modernist type… with a fire-red interior and a soaring curved section.

ARCHITECT : jesse judd

This modest three-bedroom holiday retreat, 100 kilometres northwest of Melbourne, is dominated by a startling red interior and a pronounced curved section. An alternative to the traditional Australian vernacular country home, in which materials and tectonics merge into the landscape, this house lies in a forest of tall Messmate gums (characteristic of the region) and its approach follows a winding path leading deep into the site. A first glimpse of the house reveals the architect's intent: an inflamed curved pavilion lies in wait, surrounded by the repetitive Messmate trunks. As with Philip Johnson's Glass House (1949) and Ludwig Mies van der Rohe's Farnsworth House (1946-1951), this building is raised off the ground on a broad plinth. Jesse Judd's pavilion, held taut with black steel columns, is a quirky revision of that orthogonal modernist type… with a fire-red interior and a soaring curved section.

Reading clearly as an object placed against the landscape, the dwelling is distinctly foreign, with no ambitions to harmonize with its surroundings. "This house is the landed object", states Judd, "if you want something that blends into the landscape, paint it green!" The cleared site, encircled by endless trees, provides an ideal setting for the architect to play out his ideas of the sectional geometric figure and of abrupt shifts in scale.

The entrance to the huge living room is at the end of a long conventional lean-to structure with a minimum height of 2.2 metres. As one moves into the living areas, both scale and form explode into the dramatic curve, and the space balloons out to 5.4 metres at its highest point. Following the radius of the bending structural members, the floor, walls and ceiling become one, and the interior is thus a simple extrusion of this one sectional element. This theatrical move is made all the more intense through the choice of plywood-cladding stained to an alarming orange red. The scale shift and colour are in no way subtle, and seem almost intentionally awkward. Judd describes the design as "the big ugly caravan that is towed into the pristine bush". One of his desires was to "bring something alien into the bush… that also could be described to a builder as a very simple house in plan; three bedrooms next to each other, a corridor and a big living room".

Whilst appearing initially as rather 'hard' abstract architecture, the project is not devoid of poetics, and indeed its ethereal qualities are heightened by the formal clarity. From the living room, the black columns disappear against the dark Messmate trunks, and the interior resonates with the afternoon sun's saturated warm tones. It glows brilliantly, creating a stage animated by domestic life and the variable landscape.

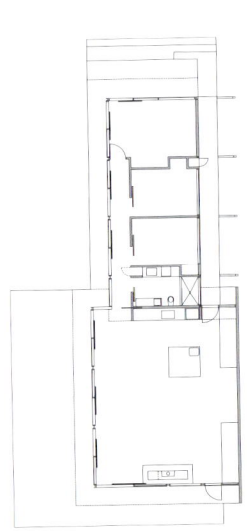

WINTER COTTAGE

As well as demonstrating a rich layering of ideas and inspirations, the **Winter Cottage** is almost entirely self-sufficient... employing a range of ecologically sustainable practices and materials.

ARCHITECT : joe chindarsi

This intricate two level residence, anchored to the side of a hilly outcrop overlooking the lush pastoral landscape surrounding Bridgetown, 260 kilometres south of Perth, is a conceptually rich dwelling of poetic and formal beauty. In its formal expression and construction, the work pays homage to the masters of modernism – Mies Van Der Rohe and Frank Lloyd Wright – but also to the memory of the previous (now demolished) residence of the owner. As well as demonstrating a rich layering of ideas and inspirations, the Winter Cottage is almost entirely self-sufficient… employing a range of ecologically sustainable practices and materials. The house is essentially a very modest structure – with three bedrooms, one bathroom and a flexible living and dining space – whose rhythmic form takes its first cues from the proportions of windows and door-frames salvaged from the owner's former residence. These are set within a Miesian expressed-steel grid, and act as the ordering device for the project's geometries and proportions. The finesse and delicacy of the architecture creates an 'inhabitable cabinet', firmly secured to the hillside with steel ties and a massive retaining wall. The northern elevation of warm timber and glass fills the house with sunlight, filtered through a screen of steel louvres set apart from the façade itself. The southern elevation takes the form of a massive gabion wall, which runs parallel to the house to create a sheltered entry passage. Joe Chindarsi cites the Dominus Winery (1999, by Herzog and de Meuron) in California, as the primary inspiration for this gesture. The regularity of the structural components and the project's orthogonal proportions intentionally form a counterpoint to the panoramic 'uncontrolled' landscape of intense climatic extremes.

The planning of the upper entry floor is organised around a central service core, and in order to extend and expand what is quite a small living area, the bedroom screen is entirely retractable. A private guest bedroom and a protected outdoor terrace are secured beneath the primary cantilevering gesture. Central to the conception and development of this house is the commitment – by both architect and owner – to sustainability and the environment. Where possible, all the materials used were local and recycled, the house incorporates a photo-voltaic array for the production of its own energy, solar hot water, a composting toilet, grey water recycling, tanks for the collection of drinking water, and all windows and doors adopt Argon-filled double-glazed units incorporating Low-E glass… Joe Chindarsi proudly observes that the ecological success of the house has pointed the way for his future projects. As time passes, the materiality of the stone, the masonry, the timber cladding and the louvres will weather and evolve, bringing the architecture of the Winter Cottage into a closer aesthetic relationship with its context.

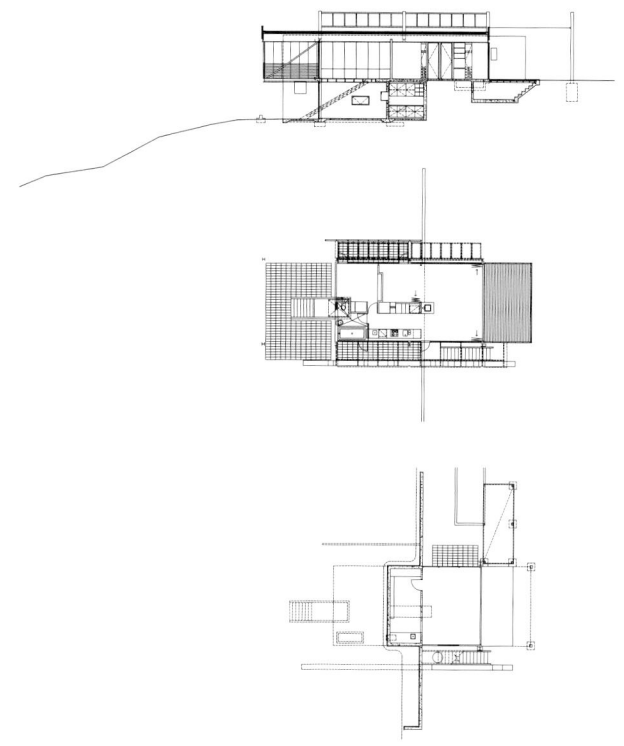

(W)RIGHT HOUSE

Nestled in the verdant splendour of Port Douglas in Far North Queensland, this house is a refreshing contemporary take on the tropical architecture idiom.

ARCHITECT : CHARLES WRIGHT

Nestled in the verdant splendour of Port Douglas in Far North Queensland, this house is a refreshing contemporary take on the tropical architecture idiom. Charles Wright brings his knowledge of helicoidal minimal surfaces, expressionist architecture and the Fibonacci golden rectangle to the challenge of building environmentally-appropriate architecture within a community overlaid with building covenants. The form – highly articulated and detailed – bends, twists and dips, both in plan and section… creating a house that is more public than domestic in its scale and expression. The intention was to provide a viable alternative to the traditional lightweight 'Queenslander' and to the 'timber and tin' vernacular, and within the context of its immediate neighbourhood, to build an alternative to the stolid neo-classical proportions of the typical resort bungalow. In contrast to the lightweight tradition, this house is more 'bunker' than 'flyaway,' and takes great delight in its display of folding abstracted lines that crack open to let in light, or that multiply and spread out to form screens covering semi-enclosed decks, water features and pools. And, as the architect intended, the house is an extraordinary object that denies any relationship with the surrounding built context, but ingeniously responds to very particular climatic conditions and to the requirements for a dwelling constantly used by an extended family.

The internal planning is generated – prosaically – by the family's desires to have a variety of living spaces that shift from the very enclosed to the very flexible, and – more poetically – by the architect's explorations of the Venturi effect, whereby the house in its entirety works as an aperture, a constricted opening that accelerates air movement throughout the interior. As the section expands and contracts along the central spine, ceilings shoot up dramatically in the living areas, directing the views to the exterior and the elaborate screening devices, whilst towards the more private areas of the house, the space compresses down to denote that programmatic shift. Brick, timber and steel are boldly and directly brought together to emphasize the fluidity of the roofline and the solidarity of the construction.

The architecture is that of a designer who revels in the paradoxical potential of constraints and regulations, but who also delights in geometric expression. Revealed in the bold heroic gesture and sophisticated sculptured interiors is a love of such architects as Alvar Aalto, John Lautner and Roy Grounds, with a wit seen more recently in the work of Ashton Raggatt McDougall and Rem Koolhaas. Glimpses of the idiosyncratic and expressionist local architecture of Eddie Oribin are also to be seen, in particular the façade of the Oribin Studio in Cairns (1963) and the soaring timber interiors of St Andrew's Presbyterian Church in Innisfail (1961). Perhaps the most notable aspect of the (w)right house, however, is the architect's unbridled delight in the possibilities provided by the hedonistic pleasures and natural affluence of Port Douglas and the Daintree region.

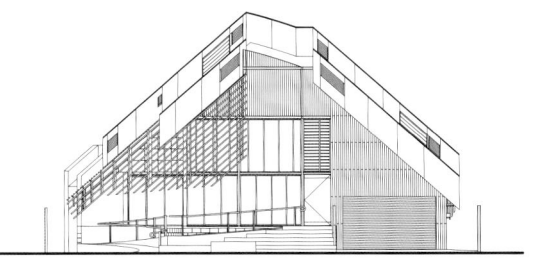

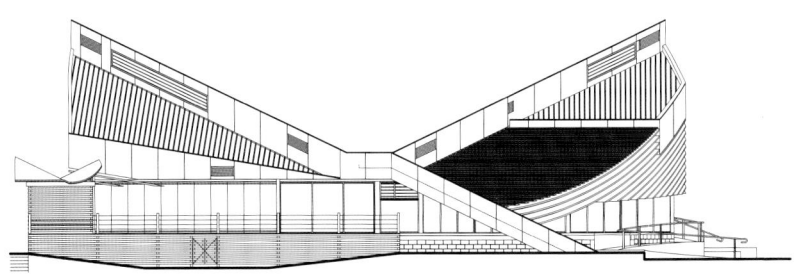

ZULAIKHA LAURENCE HOUSE

Flexibility is a characteristic of the architecture of Tonkin Zulaikha Greer (here working with Drew Heath), where a design problem is not approached with a preconceived architectural language or with a 'kit of parts', but evolves as a very direct and intimate response to the particulars of each brief.

ARCHITECT : TONKIN ZULAIKHA GREER with DREW HEATH

Perched on a site directly exposed to Sydney Harbour at the end of an East Balmain laneway, this house continues Tonkin Zulaikha Greer's investment in adaptive reuse and materiality, and in establishing a relationship with the outdoors. An old gunpowder store (dating from 1918) with bunker-like qualities had been previously converted into a house – albeit a mundane one – but the architects were more interested in the robust weighty construction and materiality of the original. These qualities were integrated into the new dwelling and, as much as possible, that original shell was maintained, with any replaced elements following the rhythms and spacing of the gunpowder store.

In contrast to the massiveness of the original, and in keeping with the architects' desire to expose the interior to the delights and drama of the Harbour, the exposed south-facing elevation is configured as a series of timber and glass screens, which are able to slide completely out of view. Attached to the outermost periphery of the building, these screens protect an extensive balcony, thus enabling the quality of the interior space to be adjusted as required. From the harbour-side, this south elevation reads like a tapestry… an abstraction of lines and textures that signifies the architects' interest in Japanese timber detailing and in 20th century modernism.

The difficulties of the site – steeply sloped and at the end of a non-trafficable lane – required non-standard delivery for all materials. The resulting cost-implications for the budget, and the architects' desire to respond efficiently to the existing constraints, resulted in a fluid design process. However, this flexibility is also a characteristic of the architecture of Tonkin Zulaikha Greer (here working with Drew Heath), where a design problem is not approached with a preconceived architectural language or with a 'kit of parts', but evolves as a very direct and intimate response to the particulars of each brief. This economy is then supplemented and enriched by the architects' love of materiality and craftsmanship. Internally, the palette of timber, plaster, concrete and glass, is stitched together in a highly orchestrated and sensuous way, as the experience moves through a rhythm of heavy roof-beams to a much more finely grained resolution of timber screens. Continuing these strategies, the spaces progress from the lower entrance to a central kitchen and dining level – clearly defined by masonry and stone enclosures – and thence to the upper level – defined by more porous and flexible threshold conditions – of the balcony, living room and bedroom. To be in this house is to be directly connected to the climatic and dramatic extremes of Sydney Harbour, whilst being protected by an architectural envelope of contrasting materials and mass.

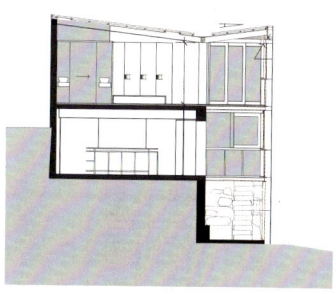
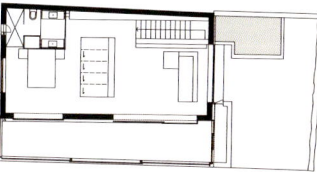
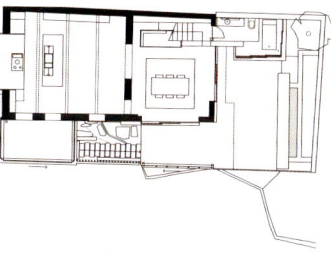

HOUSES

Adey House
Somers, VIC
Architect: Ashton Raggatt McDougall
Year of Completion: 2005

Applecross House
Applecross, Perth, WA
Architect: Jackson Clements Burrows Pty Ltd
Year of Completion: 2006
*2007 RAIA (WA) Laminex Residential
Architecture Award*
2007 RAIA (WA) George Temple Poole Award

Barro House
Kew, Melbourne, VIC
Architect: Wood Marsh
Year of Completion: 2003
2004 RAIA (VIC) Residential Architecture Award
*2004 RAIA (National) Commendation for
Residential Buildings*

Bastian Farm-House
Auburn, Clare Valley, SA
Architect: Troppo Architects
Year of Completion: 2004

Bellevue Hill House
Bellevue Hill, Sydney, NSW
Architect: Marsh Cashman Koolloos Architects
Year of Completion: 2008

Bondi Wave House
Bondi Beach, Sydney, NSW
Architect: Tony Owen NDM
Year of Completion: 2006

Box House
Tanja, NSW
Architect: Neeson Murcutt Architects
Year of Completion: 1999
2002 RAIA (NSW) Commendation

Brett's House
Rocky Hills, TAS
Architect: Rosevear Architects
Year of Completion: 2005
2005 RAIA (TAS) Architecture Award
2006 RAIA (TAS) Triennial Award

Brookes Street House
Fortitude Valley, Brisbane, QLD
Architect: James Russell Architect
Year of Completion: 2005
*2006 RAIA (QLD) Robin Dods Award for
Residential Buildings
2006 RAIA (QLD) Residential Buildings
Individual House Award
2006 RAIA (National) Commendation
for Residential Buildings*

Cape Schanck House
Cape Schanck, VIC
Architect: Paul Morgan Architects
Year of Completion: 2006
*2007 RAIA (VIC) Winner Residential
Architecture – Houses Award, Residential Category
2007 RAIA (National) Winner Robin Boyd Award for
Residential Architecture*

Cape Schanck House & Studio
Cape Schanck, VIC
Architect: Denton Corker Marshall
Year of Completion: 1999
*2000 RAIA (VIC) Merit Award Residential - New
2000 RAIA (National) Award for Most Outstanding
Residential Architecture*

Coldstream Residence
Coldstream, VIC
Architect: Allan Powell Architects
Year of Completion: 1997

Eyelid House
South Yarra, Melbourne, VIC
Architect: Fiona Winzar Architects
Year of Completion: 2006
*2007 RAIA (VIC) Winner Residential Architecture Houses
Award*

Folded House
Bronte, Sydney, NSW
Architect: Dale Jones-Evans Pty Ltd Architecture
Year of Completion: 2003

Garden House
Seaforth, Sydney, NSW
Architect: Peter Stutchbury Architecture
Year of Completion: 2007
*2008 AIA (NSW) Architecture
Award Residential Architecture*

Gidgegannup Residence
Gidgegannup, WA
Architect: iredale pedersen hook architects
Year of Completion: 2008

The Great Wall of Warburton
Warburton, VIC
Architect: BKK Architects
Year of Completion: 2008

Highgate Hill Residence
Highgate Hill, Brisbane, QLD
Architect: Richard Kirk Architect
Year of Completion: 2007

Holman House
Dover Heights, Sydney, NSW
Architect: Durbach Block Architects
Year of Completion: 2004
*2005 RAIA (NSW) Wilkinson Award for
Residential Architecture
2005 RAIA (National) Award for Housing*

House 42
Leabrook, Adelaide, SA
Architect: Dimitty Andersen Architects
Year of Completion: 2007
*2007 RAIA (SA) Award of Merit
Residential Category*

House of Orange
Clayfield, Brisbane, QLD
Architect: Elizabeth Watson-Brown Architects
Year of Completion: 2005
*2008 RAIA (Brisbane) Regional Commendation
2008 AIA (QLD) State Architecture Award Small Project
Architecture*

Ivanhoe House
Ivanhoe, Melbourne, VIC
Architect: Kerstin Thompson Architects
Year of Completion: 2008

James Robertson House
Great Mackerel Beach, Sydney, NSW
Architect: Casey Brown Architecture
Year of Completion: 2004
2004 RAIA (NSW) Architecture Award
2004 RAIA (National) Commendation

Klein Bottle House
Rye, VIC
Architect: McBride Charles Ryan
Year of Completion: 2007
2008 AIA (VIC) Harold Desbrowe-Annear Award – Residential New

Leura House
Leura, Blue Mountains, NSW
Architect: James Stockwell Architect
Year of Completion: 2007
2008 AIA (NSW) Wilkinson Award for Residential Architecture

Machans Beach Cottage
Machans Beach, Cairns, QLD
Architect: Deb Fisher, Fisher Buttrose Architects
Year of Completion: 2005
2006 RAIA (QLD) Residential Architecture Alterations & Additions
2006 RAIA (Far North QLD) House Of The Year Award

Na's House
Brookfield, Brisbane, QLD
Architect: Elizabeth Watson-Brown Architects
Year of Completion: 2007

Narveno Court House
Hawthorn, Melbourne, VIC
Architect: McBride Charles Ryan
Year of Completion: 2005
2005 RAIA (VIC) New Residential Architecture Award

Northbridge House
Northbridge, Sydney, NSW
Architect: Alex Popov Architects Pty Ltd
Year of Completion: 2004
2005 RAIA (NSW) Commendation for New Single Housing

Perham Residence
Darlinghurst, Sydney, NSW
Architect: Simon Hanson, Bureau SRH Pty Ltd
Year of Completion: 2005

Point Piper House
Point Piper, Sydney, NSW
Architect: Louise Nettleton Architects
Year of Completion: 2004
2005 RAIA (NSW) Commendation Award Single Housing – Alterations and Additions

Rosebery House
Highgate Hill, Brisbane, QLD
Architect: Andresen O'Gorman
Year of Completion: 1998

Rowntree Street House
Balmain, Sydney, NSW
Architect: Rex Addison, Addison Associates Pty Ltd
Year of Completion: 2002

Springwater
Seaforth, Sydney, NSW
Architect: Peter Stutchbury Architecture
Year of Completion: 2002
2005 RAIA (NSW) Architecture Award: Single Housing
2005 RAIA (National) Robin Boyd Award

Spry House
Point Piper, Sydney, NSW
Architect: Durbach Block Architects
Year of Completion: 2004
2004 RAIA (NSW) Architecture Award for Residential Architecture
2004 RAIA (National) Robin Boyd Award for Residential Architecture

Stanwell Park House
Stanwell Park, NSW
Architect: Casey Brown Architecture
Year of Completion: 2007

Swan Street Residence
Mosman Park, Perth, WA
Architect: iredale pedersen hook architects
Year of Completion: 2008

Tibet Gallery
Woollahra, Sydney, NSW
Architect: Donovan Hill
Year of Completion: 2003
2004 RAIA (NSW) Single Housing – Alterations & Additions Award
2004 RAIA (NSW) Conservation and Adaptive Reuse Award

Tyson Street House
Richmond, Melbourne, VIC
Architect: Jackson Clements Burrows Pty Ltd
Year of Completion: 2005

Vineyard House
Mornington, VIC
Architect: John Wardle Architects
Year of Completion: 2003
2004 RAIA (VIC) Harold Desbrowe-Annear Award for Best Residential Building

Wallaby Way House
Horseshoe Bay, Magnetic Island, QLD
Architect: Troppo Architects Queensland
Year of Completion: 2007
2008 AIA Regional Commendation

Whale Beach House
Whale Beach, Sydney, NSW
Architect: Alex Popov Architects Pty Ltd
Year of Completion: 2006

Wheatsheaf House
Daylesford, VIC
Architect: Jesse Judd, Judd Lysenko Marshall Architects
Year of Completion: 2005
2005 RAIA (VIC) Architecture Awards – Winner: Residential - New

Winter Cottage
Bridgetown, WA
Architect: Chindarsi Architects Pty Ltd
Year of Completion: 2005
2006 RAIA (WA) Ecological Sustainable Development - Architecture Award
2006 RAIA (WA) Single Residential Award - Commendation
2006 RAIA (WA) Bluescope Steel Award – Commendation
2006 RAIA (WA) Mondo-Luce Lighting Award - Commendation

(w)right House
Port Douglas, QLD
Architect: Charles Wright Architects Pty Ltd
Year of Completion: 2007
2008 AIA (Far North Queensland) Regional Commendation

Zulaikha Laurence House
Balmain East, Sydney, NSW
Architect: Tonkin Zulaikha Greer in collaboration with Drew Heath
Year of Completion: 2006
2007 RAIA (NSW) Residential Alterations and Additions Award
2007 RAIA (National) Award for Residential Architecture - Houses

(RAIA refers to the Royal Australian Institute Architects, which was renamed AIA in July 2008)

ARCHITECTS

Rex Addison
16 Stumers Road
Mt Crosby QLD 4306
Tel: +61 (0) 7 3201 1327
Fax: +61 (0) 7 3201 0237
Email: rex@ozemail.com.au
www.rexaddison.com.au

Dimitty Andersen Architects
221 Gilbert Street
Adelaide SA 5000
Tel: +61 (0) 8 8211 9649
Fax: +61 (0) 8 8211 9629
Email: dimitty@dimitty.com
www.dimitty.com

Andresen O'Gorman
9 Ormond Terrace
Indooroopilly QLD 4068

Ashton Raggatt McDougall
Level 11, 522 Flinders Lane
Melbourne VIC 3000
Tel: +61 (0) 3 8613 1888
Fax: +61 (0) 3 8613 1889
www.a-r-m.com.au

BKK Architects
Level 9, 180 Russell St
Melbourne VIC 3000
Tel: +61 (0) 3 9671 4555
Fax: +61 (0) 3 9671 4666
www.b-k-k.com.au

Simon Hanson - Bureau SRH
Studio 3, 2 Verona Street
Paddington NSW 2021
Tel: +61 (0) 2 9380 4666
Fax: +61 (0) 2 9380 4699
www.bureausrh.com

Casey Brown Architecture
Level 1, 63 William Street
East Sydney NSW 2010
Tel: +61 (0) 2 9360 7977
Fax: +61 (0) 2 9360 2123
Email: cb@caseybrown.com.au
www.caseybrown.com.au

Chindarsi Architects
73 Smith Street
Highgate WA 6003
Tel: +61 (0) 8 9328 7238
Fax: +61 (0) 8 9328 7268
www.chindarsi.com

Denton Corker Marshall
49 Exhibition Street
Melbourne VIC 3000
Tel: +61 (0) 3 9012 3600
Fax: +61 (0) 3 9012 3601
www.dentoncorkermarshall.com

Donovan Hill
112 Bowen Street
Spring Hill QLD 4000
Tel: +61 (0) 7 3831 3255
Fax: +61 (0) 7 3831 3266
Email: mail@donovanhill.com.au
www.donovanhill.com.au

Drew Heath Architects
Tel: +61 (0) 414 491 270
Email: drewheath@optusnet.com.au
www.drewheath.com.au

Durbach Block Architects
Level 5, 71 York Street
Sydney NSW 2000
Tel: +61 (0) 2 8297 3500
Fax: +61 (0) 2 8297 3510
Email: mail@durbachblock.com
www.durbachblock.com

Deb Fisher
Fisher Buttrose Architects
Level 1, 116 Grafton Street
Cairns QLD 4870
Tel: +61 (0) 7 4031 1707
Fax: +61 (0) 7 4041 5881
www.fabarchitects.com.au

iredale pedersen hook architects
Murray Mews, 329–331 Murray Street
Perth WA 6000
Tel: +61 (0) 8 9322 9750
Fax: +61 (0) 8 9322 9752
www.iredalepedersenhook.com

Jackson Clements Burrows Pty Ltd
1 Harwood Place
Melbourne VIC 3000
Tel: +61 (0) 3 9654 6227
Fax: +61 (0) 3 9654 6195
Email: jacksonclementsburrows@jcba.com.au
www.jcba.com.au

Dale Jones-Evans Pty Ltd Architecture
Loft 1, 50-54 Ann Street
Surry Hills NSW 2010
Tel: +61 (0) 2 9211 0626
Fax: +61 (0) 2 9211 5998
Email: dje@dje.com.au
www.dje.com.au

Jesse Judd
Judd Lysenko Marshall Architects
7 Glenard Drive
Eaglemont VIC 3084
Tel: +61 (0) 411 214 832
Fax: +61 (0) 3 9459 2848
Email: info@jlma.com.au
www.jlma.com.au

Richard Kirk Architect
13 Manning Street
South Brisbane QLD 4101
Tel: +61 (0) 7 3255 2526
Fax: +61 (0) 7 3255 2527
Email: mail@richardkirkarchitect.com
www.richardkirkarchitect.com

McBride Charles Ryan
Unit 4, 21 Wynnstay Road
Prahran VIC 3181
Tel: +61 (0) 3 9510 1006
Fax: +61 (0) 3 9510 0205
Email: mail@mcbridecharlesryan.com.au
www.mcbridecharlesryan.com.au

Marsh Cashman Koolloos Architects Pty Ltd
Level 4, 104 Commonwealth Street
Surry Hills NSW 2010
Tel: +61 (0) 2 9211 4146
Fax: +61 (0) 2 9211 4148
Mobile: +61 (0) 412 292 035
www.mckarchitects.com

Paul Morgan Architects
Level 10, 221 Queen St
Melbourne VIC 3000
Tel: +61 (0) 3 9600 3253
Fax: +61 (0) 3 9602 5673
Email: office@paulmorganarchitects.com
www.paulmorganarchitects.com

Neeson Murcutt Architects
Level 5, 71 York Street
Sydney NSW 2000
Tel: +61 (0) 2 8297 3590
Fax: +61 (0) 2 8297 3510
www.neesonmurcutt.com

Louise Nettleton Architects
70 Buckingham Street
Surry Hills NSW 2010
Tel: +61 (0) 2 9318 0428
Fax: +61 (0) 2 9318 2419
Email: mail@nettletonarchitect.com

Tony Owen NDM
260 Young Street
Annandale 2038 NSW
Tel: +61 (0) 2 9571 1700
Fax: +61 (0) 2 9571 1722
Email: info@tonyowen.com.au
www.tonyowen.com.au

Alex Popov Architects Pty Ltd
2 Glen Street
Milsons Point NSW 2061
Tel: +61 (0) 2 9955 5604
Fax: +61 (0) 2 9955 9258
Email: info@alexpopov.com.au
www.alexpopov.com.au

Allan Powell Architects
19 Victoria Street
St Kilda VIC 3182
Tel: +61 (0) 3 9534 8367
Fax: +61 (0) 3 9525 3615
Email: allan@allanpowell.com.au
www.allanpowell.com.au

Rosevear Architects
215, 86 Murray Street
Hobart TAS 7005
Tel: +61 (0) 3 6223 4471
Fax: +61 (0) 3 6223 3385
Email: hobart@rosevearchitects.com
www.rosevearchitects.com

James Russell Architect
116 Brookes Street
Fortitude Valley QLD 4006
Tel: +61 (0) 7 3257 0818
Email: james@jamesrussellarchitect.com.au
www.jamesrussellarchitect.com.au

James Stockwell Architect
307, 133 Goulburn Street
Surry Hills NSW 2010
Tel: +61 (0) 414 504 720
www.jamesstockwell.com.au

Peter Stutchbury Architecture
Unit 5, 364 Barrenjoey Road
Newport NSW 2106
Tel: +61 (0) 2 9979 5030
Fax: +61 (0) 2 9979 5367
Email: info@stutchburyandpape.com.au
www.stutchburyandpape.com.au

Kerstin Thompson Architects
54 Charles Street
Fitzroy VIC 3065
Tel: +61 (0) 3 9419 4969
Fax: +61 (0) 3 9419 4483
Email: kta@kerstinthompson.com
www.kerstinthompson.com

Tonkin Zulaikha Greer Architects
117 Reservoir Street
Surry Hills NSW 2010
Tel: +61 (0) 2 9215 4900
Fax: +61 (0) 2 9215 4901
Email: brian@tzg.com.au
www.tzg.com.au

Troppo Architects
28 East Terrace
Adelaide SA 5000
Tel: +61 (0) 8 8232 9696
Email: adelaide@troppoarchitects.com.au
www.troppoarchitects.com.au

Troppo Architects Queensland
7 Woolcock Street
Hyde Park, Townsville QLD 4812
Tel: +61 (0) 7 4772 4251
Fax: +61 (0) 7 4772 4252
Email: townsville@troppoarchitects.com.au
www.troppoarchitects.com.au

John Wardle Architects
Level 10, 180 Russell Street
Melbourne VIC 3000
Tel: +61 (0) 3 9654 8700
Fax: +61 (0) 3 9654 8755
Email: johnwardle@johnwardle.com
www.johnwardle.com

Elizabeth Watson-Brown Architects
22 Shaw Street
Auchenflower QLD 4066
Tel: +61 (0) 7 3870 7760
Fax: +61 (0) 7 3870 4752
Email: info@ewbarchitects.com
www.ewbarchitects.com

Fiona Winzar Architects
1, 03 The George
129 Fitzroy Street
St Kilda VIC 3182
Tel: +61 (0) 3 9593 6464
Fax: +61 (0) 3 9593 6465
www.fionawinzar.com

Wood Marsh
30 Beaconsfield Parade
Port Melbourne VIC 3207
Tel: +61 (0) 3 9676 2600
Fax: +61 (0) 3 9676 2811
Email: wm@woodmarsh.com.au
www.woodmarsh.com.au

Charles Wright Architects Pty Ltd
Shop 5, Laxmi Centre
48 Macrossan Street
Port Douglas QLD 4877
Tel: +61 (0) 7 4099 4965
Fax: +61 (0) 7 4099 4963
Email: charles@wrightarchitects.com.au
www.wrightarchitects.com.au

Editor: Patrick Bingham-Hall
Design: Pesaro Publishing & Ayeemm Cabales

All photography © Patrick Bingham-Hall & Pesaro Publishing 2008
Text © Anna Johnson and Pesaro Publishing 2008

Pesaro Publishing
PO Box 74
Balmain NSW 2041
Australia

Pesaro Publishing
14 Robinson Road #13-00
Far East Finance Building
Singapore 048545

www.pesaropublishing.com

National Library of Australia Cataloguing-in-Publication entry

Author: Johnson, Anna.

Title: The Australian House / Anna Johnson, Patrick Bingham-Hall.

ISBN: 9781877015250 (pbk.)

Subjects: Architecture--Australia.
            Architecture, Domestic--Australia.
            Dwellings--Australia.

Other Authors/Contributors: Bingham-Hall, Patrick.

Dewey Number: 728.0994

First published in 2008 by Pesaro Publishing

All rights reserved. No part of this publication may be reproduced, stored in, or introduced to, a retrieval system or transmitted in any form or by any means, electronic, mechanical, photocopying, recording or otherwise, without the prior written permission of the publishers.

ISBN 978-1-877015-25-0

Printed by CS Graphics Singapore Pte Ltd

OME RECENT AUST
EXT OF THE SITE, WH
ROM A RETHINKING
URE SHOULD LOOK L
ND DEFIANT. A MAR
ETURN TO THE IDEA
RALIA'S DOMESTIC AR
ASSIVE, IS RESOLVED
EXT, RATHER THAN

alian house desig
ilst the formal exp
of what environm
ke... and the new
ked emphasis upo
of 'architecture a
chitecture. Form
and expressed a
being synthesized